CW01457311

SNAP SCIENCE

GET YOUR TEETH INTO IT!

Teacher's Guide
Year 1

William Collins' dream of knowledge for all began with the publication of his first book in 1819.
A self-educated mill worker, he not only enriched millions of lives, but also founded a flourishing publishing house.
Today, staying true to this spirit, Collins books are packed with inspiration, innovation and practical expertise.
They place you at the centre of a world of possibility and give you exactly what you need to explore it

Published by Collins
An imprint of HarperCollins*Publishers*

The News Building, 1 London Bridge Street, London, SE1 9GF, UK

Macken House, 39/40 Mayor Street Upper, Dublin 1, D01 C9W8, Ireland

Browse the complete Collins catalogue at
collins.co.uk

© HarperCollins*Publishers* Limited 2024

10 9 8 7 6 5 4 3 2 1

ISBN 978-0-00-868517-1

All rights reserved. No part of this publication may be reproduced, stored in a retrieval system, or transmitted in
any form by any means, electronic, mechanical, photocopying, recording or otherwise, without the prior written permission of the Publisher or a licence permitting restricted copying in the United Kingdom issued by the
Copyright Licensing Agency Ltd, 5th Floor, Shackleton House, 4 Battle Bridge Lane, London SE1 2HX.

British Library Cataloguing-in-Publication Data

A catalogue record for this publication is available from the British Library.

Authors: David Allen, Nicola Beverley, Naomi Hiscock, Liz Lawrence, Jules Pottle and Claire Seeley
Series Editor: Jane Turner
Publisher: Laura White
Packager: Oriel Square
Cover designer: Amparo at Kneath Associates
Production controller: Alhady Ali

Printed and Bound in the UK by Ashford Colour Press Ltd

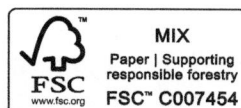

MIX
Paper | Supporting responsible forestry
FSC
www.fsc.org   FSC™ C007454

This book contains FSC™ certified paper and other controlled sources to ensure responsible forest management.

For more information visit: www.harpercollins.co.uk/green

Acknowledgements

The publishers gratefully acknowledge the permission granted to reproduce the copyright material in this book. Every effort has been made to trace copyright holders and to obtain their permission for the use of copyright material. The publishers will gladly receive any information enabling them to rectify any error or omission at the first opportunity.

Contents

Introduction to *Snap Science*

What is *Snap Science*?

Snap Science is a comprehensive and rich resource that provides everything primary schools need to plan, teach and assess the National Curriculum for primary science. It has been written by a team of leading experts who have spent years teaching science in primary schools, working with trainees, delivering professional learning for teachers and subject leaders, carrying out research, developing resources and advising policy makers and curriculum designers. Each of them is passionate about primary science: they know how important it is for primary children to develop secure knowledge of the big ideas in science, to learn how scientists work to build that knowledge and how that knowledge can be used to meet the global changes we face. They know how exciting it is to be in a primary classroom when science is being well taught: where children are connecting their learning, finding things out through practical experimentation, using scientific vocabulary to explain what they know and seeing the relevance of their learning to their lives.

They also know how challenging it is to lead and teach primary science well, and what a responsibility that is. It is not easy to plan a curriculum which is made up of complex ideas in Biology, Chemistry and Physics as well as the disciplinary knowledge of working scientifically, which includes practical work and outdoor learning, and which needs to build positive attitudes as well as secure learning.

So that is why they created *Snap* – to give teachers the resources that will develop the confidence, skills and knowledge to teach science well.

What is the *Snap* framework?

- A complete long-term plan for science which fully covers the National Curriculum and is constructed to ensure clear progression of knowledge and skills year by year.

- Medium-term plans for each year group, organised as six modules where the learning has been broken into straightforward, cognitively appropriate steps to be taught and assessed lesson by lesson.

- Between four and eight lesson plans per module.

- Resources to support teachers to plan, teach and assess science effectively.

- The realisation of the *Snap* vision for science: for all children to make sustained progress, securely learning new knowledge and skills and connecting then to prior learning, exploring the world through practical experimentation, building positive attitudes to science and seeing the relevance of their learning to their lives and how it can help build a better future for all.

How has the long-term plan been designed?

The *Snap* long-term plan provides subject leaders with a coherent curriculum for science, from Year 1 to Year 6. The National Curriculum has been broken into modules which are organised logically to ensure that all substantive and disciplinary knowledge is taught and learnt well, at an appropriate time of the year and in an order which is underpinned by a clear progression. Scientific ideas, skills and vocabulary have all been sequenced to make sure that children's learning builds on prior understanding.

What are *Snap* lessons like?

Each lesson is framed by a question – often a science enquiry question. In the lesson, children are taught new knowledge to enable them to answer that question. In many lessons they also collect data using an enquiry type to help then answer the question. In each lesson, formative assessment strategies are used to elicit children's prior knowledge, so that learning is progressive. Every lesson ends with a 'reflect and review' activity where children summarise their learning.

Each lesson is designed to teach a part of or a complete National Curriculum substantive knowledge statement, and for children to make progress towards meeting relevant working scientifically statements. Assessment indicators are provided to enable teachers and children to make accurate judgements about the progress that has been made.

Enquiry types are used appropriately, and working scientifically skills are explicitly taught and used, with clear links made to how scientists, including named historical and contemporary figures, work.

Clear guidance for teachers is provided to use a range of evidence-informed teaching strategies, including practical work, use of Tier 3 vocabulary, teacher demonstration, direct teaching, enquiry-based learning, modelling, drama, outdoor learning, and dialogic teaching.

Practical, logistical information is included about timing, teaching spaces and equipment.

Teaching is enriched with videos, interactives, slide shows, resource sheets and images. Learning activities are clearly outlined and resources are provided for collecting data, recording observation and summarising learning.

What other support for subject leaders and teachers is there?

The *Snap* Pupil Workbooks and printed Teacher's Guides can be used alongside the *Snap* digital subscription available on Collins Hub. As well as editable versions of the lesson plans in this book, there are module summaries, PowerPoints, videos, animations, assessments and resource sheets, and comprehensive teacher support and CPD.

What is in each module summary?

Each module contains everything a teacher needs to teach a topic.

The **National Curriculum statements** taught in each module have been broken into a detailed progression of learning. The science that children will learn in each lesson is clearly stated as well as how teachers will assess that learning, using evidence from what children do in the lesson. There are additional assessment activities called Snapshots that teachers can use if they are unable to make an assessment judgement based on what children write, say, draw or model in the classroom.

The **subject knowledge** teachers need to make sure that their own understanding is strong and their explanations are accurate is included. Scientific misconceptions children (and teachers) may hold are listed with the correct version given. The **scientific vocabulary** (Tier 3) that children will learn and use in the lessons is listed with age-appropriate definitions, as well as any non-science specific words (Tier 2) that may be needed to fully engage with the lesson.

Vital information is included to guide teachers to teach in ways that will build all children's **science capital**, valuing children's knowledge, ideas and experiences, and developing their capacity to use their science learning in their lives now and in the future. Meaningful **links to other subject areas** are made, including carefully selected books for children to read to enhance their science learning. Full **resource lists**, created to be sustainable, affordable and meet health and safety guidance are included.

What support is there for science leaders?

Leading science using *Snap* is a useful summary of how *Snap Science* enables confident and enjoyable leadership of science. Read this for information about how *Snap* supports subject leaders to meet Ofsted 2023 recommendations for curriculum design, progression and best practice in teaching, learning and assessment in their school.

For further information about the *Snap* approach there are briefings to explain the *Snap* understanding of best practice science teaching and learning and what has informed it. These summarise current evidence-based guidance about **Working scientifically, Assessment, Sustainability, Equality, diversity and inclusion** and **Integrating literacy**. These are also available as short, summary presentations which you can use in staff meetings.

The *Snap* long-term plan shows how the National Curriculum is organised for Years 1–6. The *Snap* Progression charts for Conceptual knowledge and Working scientifically provide a lot more detail. Planning using *Snap* and Teaching and assessing using *Snap* are important documents to share with teachers as they provide full guidance for using the *Snap* framework. These are also available as ten-minute summary presentations which you can use in staff meetings.

There are also examples of Module summaries and Lesson plans with quick-reference annotations explaining how to use the guidance in the different sections.

The *Snap* assessment trackers, one per year, enable teachers to track children's progress easily throughout the year, and are presented as Excel spreadsheets so that you can integrate information with your school's own systems if necessary. Instructions for using it are in Teaching and assessing using Snap.

The Glossaries of the science-specific vocabulary, one for each year, are useful reference documents for teachers, giving simple definitions for each word appropriate to the year, with progression baked in.

The Resources lists will make sure that everyone is well prepared with everything they need to teach great lessons.

Lesson overview

Lesson	Workbook page
Module 1: Seasonal changes	
Lesson 1: Are all leaves the same? (September) Leaves vary in colour, texture and shape. Leaves can be used to help identify plants.	*2–4*
Lesson 2: Which animals share our space? (autumn) Different animals have different habitats. In autumn the weather becomes colder, leaves change colour, daylight hours become shorter.	*5–7*
Lesson 3: Do all trees shed their leaves? (early winter) Deciduous leaves change colour in the autumn and fall to the ground. Evergreen trees do not drop their leaves. Winter is the season that comes after autumn. It has the coldest weather of the year. It is less easy to see insects and mammals in winter.	*8–10*
Lesson 4: Are all flowers the same? (spring) Flowers vary by shape and colour. Different plants flower at different times of the year. There are more flowering plants in the spring and summer. In spring the temperature and the number of daylight hours begin to increase, plants begin to grow and hibernating animals emerge.	*11–13*
Lesson 5: Which birds can we spot? (spring) There are signs of animals in every school grounds. Different types of birds can be seen at different times of the year. Most insects can be seen in the spring and summer.	*14–17*
Lesson 6: How has our space changed over the year? (early summer) Summer is the warmest season of the year. The sun is highest in the sky in the summer. Many flowering plants produce fruits in the summer. Common natural events can be matched to the seasons. For example, leaf buds and blossoms with spring; fruit formation with summer; leaf drop with autumn and animal hibernation with winter.	*18–21*
Module 2: Human body and senses	
Lesson 1: Is everyone's body the same? Humans are mammals and vertebrates. The main parts of the human body are head, arms and hands, torso, and legs and feet. We also have five basic senses which help us to make sense of the world around us. One of these is sight and our eyes give us the capacity to see. Although humans are all the same generally, they vary in, for example, their skin, hair, eye colour, shoe size and fingerprint.	*22–24*
Lesson 2: How can we explore the world using our sense of touch? Touch is another human sense which helps us to stay safe. Hands and feet are the most commonly used parts of the body to touch and explore the world around us, but other parts can be used too.	*25–27*

Lesson 3: What can we hear? Our ears are the part of our body that hears, and this is another human sense.	*28–29*
Lesson 4: What smells do we like and dislike? The nose is the part of the human body associated with smell, another human sense.	*30–31*
Lesson 5: What differences can our tongues taste? The human sense of taste uses the tongue to detect the flavour of what is in our mouths and can help us decide if we like a food or not. This sense is looked at last in the conceptual order because it is a way to connect other senses together. Taste is supported by the senses of smell, touch and sight.	*32–33*
Module 3: Naming and describing materials	
Lessons 1 and 2: What material is this? Parts 1 and 2 Everything around us is made from materials. Some materials are natural materials, naturally sourced materials that are used without modification. Some materials are manufactured materials, made by changing naturally sourced materials. Different materials have different properties. Materials should be used carefully and can often be reused or recycled.	*34–36* *37–39*
Lesson 3: Is all paper the same? Paper is a manufactured material made from wood, which is a natural material. Different types of paper have different properties and uses. Some paper can be recycled.	*40–41*
Lesson 4: Is all fabric the same? Fabric is a manufactured material which can be made wholly or partly from different source materials and therefore there are different types of fabric with different properties. Different types of fabric have different properties and uses. Fabrics can be made from recycled materials and should be reused or recycled whenever possible.	*42–43*
Lesson 5: How can we group objects made of different materials? Objects can be sorted according to their source material, and as natural and manufactured. Objects can be made from more than one material.	*44–46*
Module 4: Properties and uses of materials	
Lesson 1: Can the same object be made from different materials? Objects are made from one or more materials. Objects can be sorted in various ways, including by type of material or function/purpose. Materials should be used carefully, can often be reused and some can be recycled.	*47–48*
Lesson 2: What properties do materials have? Materials have physical properties that make them useful for different purposes.	*49–50*
Lesson 3: Does it bend or stretch? Some materials can be bent or stretched, making them useful for particular purposes.	*51–52*
Lesson 4: Do all materials get wet? Some materials are absorbent, 'soaking up' liquid on contact and some materials are waterproof, making them useful for particular purposes.	*53–54*

Module 5: Animals (vertebrates)

Lesson 1: Who's who in the animal (vertebrate) world? There are five vertebrate groups in the animal kingdom: mammals, amphibians, reptiles, birds and fish. Reptiles are one of these, and the things that make them distinct are: eggs, claws, teeth, scaly skin and living on land.	*55–56*
Lesson 2: What's so special about birds? Birds are vertebrates and the things that make them distinct are: eggs, beaks, claws, wings and feathers.	*57–59*
Lesson 3: What makes an amphibian an amphibian? Amphibians are vertebrates and the things that make them distinct are: eggs, living on land and in water and their diet changing with their stage of life.	*60–62*
Lesson 4: Do fish have fingers? Fish are vertebrates and the things that make them distinct are: they lay eggs, they have gills to help them breathe underwater, they have fins and a tail to help them swim, and most fish have scales to protect them.	*63–65*
Lesson 5: Are humans mammals? Mammals are vertebrates and humans are mammals too. The things that make mammals distinct are: hair or fur covering their bodies, giving birth to live young, producing milk for offspring, nurturing offspring, looking like a younger version of their parent and having a range of movement.	*66–68*

Module 6: Identifying plants and their parts

Lesson 1: What wild and garden plants can we find around our school? Wild and garden plants can be found around the school and locality, including flowering plants, and these can be identified and named.	*69–70*
Lesson 2: What parts of a plant grow above the ground? The names of the parts of a flowering plant that grow above the ground are the stem, leaf, and flower.	*71*
Lesson 3: What part of a plant grows under the ground? Roots grow under the ground and different plants have different roots.	*72–73*
Lesson 4: Why are trees plants? Trees are plants which have roots, stems, leaves and most have flowers. There are differences between deciduous and evergreen trees.	*74–75*
Lesson 5: What are the similarities and differences between plants that have flowers? There are similarities and differences between flowering plants.	*76–77*

Module 1: Seasonal changes

Lesson 1: Are all leaves the same?

This lesson should be taught in September.

What children will learn and do

- Children explore and become familiar with an outdoor space that they will return to throughout the year.
- They notice and record the weather conditions.
- They sort leaves according to colour, texture and shape.
- They learn that differences in leaves can be used to help identify plants.
- They answer the lesson question: **'Are all leaves the same?'**

You will need

- to prepare the children to work outside
- to identify an outdoor space that the children can return to throughout the year, containing variety of plants including trees, flowers and space for a bird feeder
- cones to mark the outdoor work space
- a selection of leaves from the outdoor space, the children will be matching these leaves to the plants in your space
- crayons
- clipboards
- paper for leaf rubbings
- camera
- a hoop (sorting hoop or PE hula hoop)
- mini whiteboard and pen

If using the Snap Science Year 1 Pupil Workbook you may not require all of the resource sheets below.

Snap Science Year 1 Pupil Workbook

- pages 2–4

Snap Science Year 1 Digital subscription

- My Seasons Diary (printed and stapled together)
- Resource sheet 1: Leaf ID sheet (optional)
- Resource sheet 2: Weather symbols ID cards

Make sure you have opened/printed any *Snap* resources you intend to use in this lesson.

National Curriculum

Conceptual knowledge:

- observe changes across the four seasons
- observe and describe weather associated with the seasons and how day length varies

Working scientifically:

- observing closely [using simple equipment]
- identifying and classifying

Scientific enquiry type:

- identifying and classifying

SNAP SCIENCE
GET YOUR TEETH INTO IT!
2nd EDITION

Key vocabulary	
Tier 2 vocabulary:	**Tier 3 vocabulary:**
compare, different, match, record (noun), similar	identify
	leaf/leaves, plant

Health and safety Please refer to CLEAPSS for Health and Safety guidance and ensure that any identified hazards are managed appropriately.

Getting started

This is the first of six outdoor lessons across the year. Begin by helping children to familiarise themselves with the outdoor space they will be studying. Tell children that they will be keeping a diary and that they will be visiting this area to see what changes over the year.

Each time the children go outside they will record the weather by circling a weather symbol in their My Seasons Diary. In order to introduce those symbols to the children, show them the weather symbols cards (Resource sheet 2). Ask children to tell you which type of weather the symbol represents. Ask children to tell you what the weather is like today. Ask them to circle the correct weather symbol(s) in their My Seasons Diary.

Tell children that today they are going to answer the lesson question: **'Are all leaves the same?'**

In order to answer this question, children will learn to look closely and compare leaves.

Give each child a leaf to look at closely. Ask: What shape is it? What colours can you see on it? How does it feel? Is it dull or furry like felt? Is it shiny? Is it smooth? Is it wrinkled? Does it have round edges? Does it have frilly edges? Does it have spiky edges?

Then ask them to compare their leaf with their partner. Ask them if this leaf is the same as their partner's? How are they the same? How are they different?

Pupil workbook: Complete Activity 1: Today's weather and length of day on page 2.

The task

Give each pair of children a leaf to work with. As before, ask them to look at its shape and features. Ask them to do a leaf rubbing of their leaf to add to their diary. Then challenge them to go and find the plant that matches the leaf in their hands. Help children to think about the clues they will look for. For example, leaf texture, shape, colour and size. Tell them that they may need to look at more than one plant in order to find the right match. When they find the correct plant, ask them to draw a picture of the plant in their diaries.

Pupil workbook: Complete Activity 2: My leaf on page 3 and Activity 3: Which plant did my leaf come from? on page 3.

Adaptations and support

Some children may need a simpler task. In which case they could go on a leaf safari, use Resource sheet 1: Leaf ID sheet, and tick off as many of the leaves on there as they can find.

Take it further

Ask children to see how many different leaves they can find.

Reflect and review

Review with children a few of the matches that they made. Which plants did the leaves come from? Discuss with them how they knew that the leaf came from that plant.

Remind children of the lesson question: **'Are all leaves the same?'** Ask children to discuss the answer to this question in pairs. Can they explain why all leaves are different? Children should have noticed that while the leaves on one plant may all be similar, leaves on different types of plants will be different. We can identify a plant by its leaves.

Place the hoop on the grass and place a mini whiteboard next to it with the name of a particular leaf characteristic, for example, shiny or wrinkly. Ask children to look at their leaf and to think about whether they can place it in the hoop. Then together, look at the leaves within the hoop, for example, the shiny leaves. Are they different or the same? Then repeat this activity, but this time ask children to decide on a different criteria for sorting the leaves.

Tell children that they will be revisiting this area lots of times across the year. Each time they visit they will look to see how the weather is different and what has happened to the plants they have seen today. Tell them to complete the front page of their My Seasons Diary with a photograph or drawing of a tree in the area.

Pupil workbook: Complete Activity 4: Seasonal tree on page 4.

Answers

Children should notice that leaves vary in colour, texture and shape. Leaves can be used to help identify plants.

Homework suggestions

Ask children to collect some leaves from outdoor spaces near where they live. These plants could be found on their way home from school, in the school grounds, local parks or in personal gardens. How many different types of leaves can they find? Use them to make a leaf picture – this can be created on the floor as a piece of moveable art.

Assessment and evidence of learning

Children can:

- describe in simple terms what they see
- compare the leaves, noticing their texture, colour, size, shape or smell
- state that different plants have different leaves
- match their leaf to the plant it came from.

SNAP SCIENCE
GET YOUR TEETH INTO IT!
2nd EDITION

Lesson 2: Which animals share our space?

This lesson should be taught in autumn when leaves of deciduous trees are beginning to turn brown and fall.

What children will learn and do

- Children revisit the same outdoor space as in their last seasonal change lesson to observe changes.
- They learn about the changes that occur to trees, weather and daylight hours in autumn.
- They identify and name animals found around the school.
- They learn that different animals live in different places within the school grounds.
- They learn that bird feeding stations help birds stay alive through the cold winter months.
- They answer the lesson question: **'Which animals share our space?'**

You will need

- to prepare the children to work outside
- cones to mark the outdoor work space
- clipboards
- bird feeders
- bird food

If using the Snap Science Year 1 Pupil Workbook you may not require all of the resource sheets below.

Snap Science Year 1 Pupil Workbook

- pages 5–7

Snap Science Year 1 Digital subscription

- My Seasons Diary
- Resource sheet 1: Animal ID sheet (optional)
- Resource sheet 2: Animal ID cards

Make sure you have opened/printed any *Snap* resources you intend to use in this lesson.

National Curriculum

Conceptual knowledge:

- observe changes across the four seasons
- observe and describe weather associated with the seasons and how day length varies
- identify and name a variety of common animals including fish, amphibians, reptiles, birds and mammals

Working scientifically:

- observing closely [using simple equipment]
- identifying and classifying
- gathering and recording data to help answer questions

Scientific enquiry type:

- identifying and classifying

Key vocabulary	
Tier 2 vocabulary:	**Tier 3 vocabulary:**
record	bird, season

Health and safety Please refer to CLEAPSS for Health and Safety guidance and ensure that any identified hazards are managed appropriately.

Getting started

This is the second of six outdoor lessons across the year. During the last lesson, children began to learn about the plants that occupy that space. In this session they will focus on the animals that live there.

As you did last time, begin the session by discussing the weather. Ask children to circle a weather symbol in their My Seasons Diary on the next page. Ask them to look back to their first diary entry. What was the weather like last time? How has the weather changed? Is it warmer or colder? Wetter or drier? Is it windier? Ask children what has happened to the plants in that space? Have they changed at all?

Ask children what season it is. Confirm that it is autumn, the season when it begins to get colder. There are lots of signs of autumn that they could look for. They may see tree seeds such as acorns or sycamore seeds falling on the ground. They may spot blackberries on brambles, or apples beginning to ripen. The leaves on the trees may start to change colour or animals may begin to prepare for winter by growing thicker coats or storing food.

Ask children to look around them. What has happened to the plants in this space? Have the plants changed or have they stayed the same? Ask them to give examples of the changes they can see. Can they see any signs of autumn? Ask children to complete the autumn page in their My Seasons Diary.

Tell the children that, today, they are going to answer the question: **'Which animals share our space?'** In order to answer this question, the children are going to look for signs of animals. Show the children the cards of animals that they may see, Resource sheet 2: Animal ID cards, ask the name of the animal and find out what they know about it. Where might you see it?

Pupil workbook: Complete Activity 1: Today's weather and length of day on page 5 and Activity 2: Signs of autumn on page 5.

The task

Tell the children they are going to look around the school grounds to see which animals they can see. Explain that animals can hide, so they will also need to look for clues that the animals have left behind. For example: spider webs, feathers, bird nests, nibbled pine cones (squirrels), fox den holes. It is important to explain that if the children spot animal poo they should never touch it. However, also explain that animal poos can give us valuable clues as to which animals have been around. We might find out that some animals only visit the school grounds at night!

Remind the children that they must move around the area very slowly and quietly so that they do not frighten the animals away. Ask the children to record which animals they see any sign of on the Animal Spotter page of their My Seasons Diary. Tick off any animals that they see and also any clues left behind from animals.

Before you leave the space, set up a bird feeding station with your children. Ask them to think about why feeding the birds in autumn is important. Tell children that as the weather gets colder it can be harder for animals to find all the food they need. Make sure that you regularly restock the bird feeders and keep them clean. Once you begin to feed the birds they will rely on them. Place the station in a sheltered, but open spot, away from predators. Children will look at the birds which use their space later in the module.

Pupil workbook: Complete Activity 3: Which animals live near me? on page 6.

Adaptations and support

If there are too many animals on the spotter page, you could select those most likely for their setting or the children could use Resource sheet 1: Animal ID sheet to look for fewer animals.

Take it further

Ask the children to look again in their space. Can they spot any other insects? How many do they find? Record any additional finds in their My Seasons Diary.

Reflect and review

Ask children to look at their animal spotter sheet. Which animals did they spot? Which animals did they not spot? Go through each animal and talk about where children found the animal or its clues.
Encourage children to use the structures:

There were more …

There were not many …

I found the … by the …

I found the … under the …

I did not see any …

Reflect on the lesson question: **'Which animals share our space?'** Ask children to discuss the answer to this question in pairs. Children should have noticed different animals live in different places within the school grounds. Ask them which animals they didn't see today? Ask them to think about why that may be? Talk to children about the bird feeding station. Which animals do they think will use this?

Remind children that they will be revisiting this site lots of times across the year. Each time they visit they will look to see how the weather is different and what has happened to the animals they have seen today. Ask the children which animals they think they might see on their next visit?

Pupil workbook: Complete Activity 4: What did you find on your walk? on page 7.

Answers

Children should notice that different types of animals can be found in different places. For example, they are more likely to see a woodlouse on the ground, under a log or at the base of a tree, or spider webs might be found on the outside of buildings or in shrubs.

Homework suggestions

Ask children to look out for animal clues on their way home from school. Can they spot a snail shell, a feather, a spider's web, a footprint, or a bird's nest? Encourage them to think about which animal left those clues behind.

Assessment and evidence of learning

Children can:
- identify and name a variety of common animals found around the school
- talk about where the animal was found
- explain that some objects are evidence of animal activity
- begin to identify signs of autumn and notice how the area has changed from their last visit.

SNAP
SCIENCE
GET YOUR TEETH INTO IT!
2nd EDITION

Lesson 3: Do all trees shed their leaves?

This lesson should be taught in early winter when deciduous trees have shed their leaves.

What children will learn and do

- Children revisit the same outdoor space as in their last seasonal change lesson to observe changes.

- They notice that it is less easy to see signs of insects and mammals in winter.

- They learn the difference between deciduous and evergreen trees.

- They answer the lesson question: **'Do all trees shed their leaves?'**

You will need

- to prepare the children to work outside
- cones to mark the outdoor work space
- a selection of leaves from the outdoor space for matching activities
- clipboards

If using the Snap Science Year 1 Pupil Workbook you may not require all of the resource sheets below.

Snap Science Year 1 Pupil Workbook

- pages 8–10

Snap Science Year 1 Digital subscription

- My Seasons Diary
- Resource sheet 1: What is the same? What is different? (optional)
- Resource sheet 2: Leaf ID cards

Make sure you have opened/printed any *Snap* resources you intend to use in this lesson.

National Curriculum

Conceptual knowledge:

- observe changes across the four seasons
- observe and describe weather associated with the seasons and how day length varies

Working scientifically:

- observing closely [using simple equipment]
- identifying and classifying

Scientific enquiry type:

- identifying and classifying

Key vocabulary	
Tier 2 vocabulary:	**Tier 3 vocabulary:**
compare, different, match, record	deciduous, evergreen, leaves, tree, season

Health and safety Please refer to CLEAPSS for Health and Safety guidance and ensure that any identified hazards are managed appropriately.

Getting started

This is the third of six outdoor lessons across the year. In this session children will revisit the first seasonal change lesson in which they looked at leaves. This lesson is best taught once deciduous trees have shed their leaves.

As you did last time, begin the session by discussing the weather. Ask children to circle a weather symbol in their My Seasons Diary. Ask children to look back to their last diary entry. What was the weather like last time? How has the weather changed? Is it warmer or colder? Wetter or drier? Is it windier? Ask them to think about what they are wearing. Are they wearing more clothes than last time? What extra things are they wearing?

Ask children what season it is. Confirm that it is winter. Explain that winter is the season that follows autumn and is the coldest season of the year. There are lots of signs of winter that children could look for. They may see frost on the grass, or puddles turned to ice. Ask children to look around them. Can they see any signs of winter? Children might notice bright berries on holly or rowan trees. They may notice that different birds have arrived. (In the winter many migrant species such as redwings or waxwings have arrived from other countries. There are also summer migrant birds too.) Children might also notice that there are fewer insects about in the wintertime.

Ask children what has happened to the trees in this space? Have they changed or have they stayed the same? Ask children to complete the 'My winter visit' page in their My Seasons Diary.

Tell children that today they are going to answer the lesson question: **'Do all trees shed their leaves?'**

Introduce the terms deciduous and evergreen. Children may have observed that lots of trees have lost their leaves, leaving bare branches. Explain that those trees are deciduous, which means that in the autumn their leaves change colour and fall off. By the winter the tree has no leaves on its branches. Oak, horse chestnut, beech, hawthorn and hazel are examples of deciduous trees. Most deciduous trees have wide, broad, flat leaves.

Not all trees are deciduous. Some trees that keep their leaves through the winter are called evergreen trees. These trees continually shed and replace leaves throughout the year. Holly, Scots pine, and laurel are all examples of evergreen trees.

Pupil workbook: Complete Activity 1: Today's weather and length of day on page 8 and Activity 2: Signs of winter on page 8.

The task

Children are going to go on a leaf hunt and record their findings in the Evergreen or Deciduous? sections in their My Seasons Diary.

At each tree, look up to see if it still has any leaves on it. If it does have leaves on it, try and match the leaves to the leaf ID sheet in the diary. Write the name or draw a picture of its leaves in the Evergreen box. If the tree does not have leaves on it, pick up one of its leaves from underneath the tree. Do a leaf rubbing and stick it in the deciduous box.

Pupil workbook: Complete Activity 3: Evergreen or deciduous? on pages 9 and 10.

Adaptations and support

Instead of leaf rubbing or drawing, children could try pressing the leaf into some playdough to make a leaf print. Alternatively, they can collect some leaves to make paint prints with. Take a photograph of the results and stick it into their My Seasons Diary.

Take it further

Compare either two trees in your space or two tree photos – sycamore and Scots pine on Resource sheet 1: What is the same? What is different? Discuss with children how these leaves are similar or different.

Reflect and review

Using Resource sheet 2: Leaf ID cards, ask children to sort the leaves into sets of evergreen and deciduous trees. Compare the leaves in each set. What do they notice? The deciduous leaves tend to be broader. Alternatively, look at the deciduous leaves that the children collected. Which plants did the leaves come from? What did the leaves have in common? How were they different from the leaves on the evergreen trees?

Remind children of the lesson question: **'Do all trees shed their leaves?'** Ask them to discuss the answer to this question in pairs. Ask children how we know if a tree is evergreen or deciduous? Ask children to write their answer in their diary.

Remind children that they will be revisiting this site lots of times across the year. Each time they visit they will look to see how the weather is different and how the space has changed. In the springtime they can look to see how the deciduous trees grow new leaves!

Answers

Children should recognise that a tree is evergreen because it still has its leaves in the winter. A tree is deciduous because it has lost its leaves in the winter.

Homework suggestions

On a cold winter's evening, leave shallow containers of water outside overnight and watch what happens to it. How did the water change? Try leaving containers with different amounts of water in. Does the same thing happen to all of them?

Assessment and evidence of learning

Children can:
- begin to identify signs of winter and notice how the space has changed from their last visit
- state the difference between evergreen and deciduous trees.

Lesson 4: Are all flowers the same?

This lesson should be taught in spring when there are flowers to observe.

What children will learn and do

- Children revisit the same outdoor space as in their last seasonal change lesson to observe changes.
- They learn that spring is the season where the temperatures and the amount of daylight begin to rise, plants begin to grow and hibernating animals emerge.
- They observe simple features on flowers, such as the colour and shape of petals.
- They answer the lesson question: **'Are all flowers the same?'**

You will need

- to prepare the children to work outside
- cones to mark the outdoor work space
- clipboards
- camera
- drawing paper (optional)

If using the Snap Science Year 1 Pupil Workbook you may not require the resource sheet below.

Snap Science Year 1 Pupil Workbook

- pages 11–13

Snap Science Year 1 Digital subscription

- My Seasons Diary
- Resource sheet 1: Spring flower ID cards

Make sure you have opened/printed any *Snap* resources you intend to use in this lesson.

National Curriculum

Conceptual knowledge:

- observe changes across the four seasons
- observe and describe weather associated with the seasons and how day length varies

Working scientifically:

- observing closely [using simple equipment]
- identifying and classifying

Scientific enquiry type:

- identifying and classifying

Key vocabulary	
Tier 2 vocabulary:	**Tier 3 vocabulary:**
compare, different, match, record, similar	flower, petal

Health and safety Please refer to CLEAPSS for Health and Safety guidance and ensure that any identified hazards are managed appropriately.

Getting started

This is the fourth of six outdoor lessons across the year. In this session the children will explore the diverse world of flowers, looking at their many shapes, colours and forms. This lesson builds on Module 5 Identifying plants and their parts Lesson 5, What are the similarities and differences between plants that have flowers?

Begin by discussing the weather. Ask children to circle a weather symbol in their My Seasons Diary. Ask children to look back at their diary entries. What was the weather like last time? How has the weather changed? Is it warmer or colder? Wetter or drier? Is it windier? Ask them to think about what they are wearing. Are they wearing more or fewer clothes than last time?

Ask children what season it is. Confirm that it is spring. Explain that spring is the season that follows winter. There are lots of signs of spring that they could look for.

Each type of flower has a typical bloom time. In this lesson we are looking at flowers that bloom in spring. They may see spring flowers such as snowdrops, crocuses, primroses, daffodils and bluebells. They may see blossom on trees, such as blackthorn and hawthorn.

Children will also begin to hear insects buzzing and humming as they emerge from their winter hideaways. They may have noticed that days are longer and evenings stay lighter. Birdsong may be heard, birds begin to build their nests. Ask children to look around them. What signs of spring can they see or hear?

Ask children what has happened to the trees in this space? Have they changed or have they stayed the same? Ask children to complete the signs of spring box in their My Seasons Diary.

Pupil workbook: Complete Activity 1: Today's weather and length of day on page 11 and Activity 2: Signs of spring on page 11.

The task

Tell children that today they are going to answer the lesson question: **'Are all flowers the same?'**

Show children a flower. Point out the petals. Tell them that the petals protect the inside of the flower. Some flowers have brightly coloured petals. These flowers attract insects and birds who will come and feed from them.

Show children Resource sheet 1: Spring flower ID cards. Talk about the colour and shape of each flower. For example, bluebells are blue, bell-shaped flowers. Daffodils are yellow or white, trumpet-shaped flowers while forget-me-nots are small, simple, saucer-shaped flowers. Show the children the spring flower spotter activity in their diary. Show children how to tick off when they see a flower that matches a colour on their chart.

Explain to children that flowers are important. They provide food for insects, birds and animals. So when they are working they may smell and look at the flowers, but they must not pick them.

Pupil workbook: Complete Activity 3: Comparing flowers on page 12 and Activity 4: Flower colours in spring on page 13.

Adaptations and support

Children could take photographs of different flowers that they see and use these to make a collage of spring flowers.

Take it further

Children could draw some of the flowers that they see outside. Ask children to count how many petals the flowers have and to look closely at their size and shape.

Reflect and review

Remind children of the lesson question: **'Are all flowers the same?'** Discuss the different shapes and colours of flowers that children saw. They may have observed flowers on trees and shrubs as well as on annual and perennial plants. Ask children which were the most common colour flowers in the spring? Tell children that we mainly see yellow and white flowers in very early spring. That is because they are bright, reflect lots of light and are easier for flying insects to see. Flying insects cannot see colour very easily. Ask children to answer the question in their diary.

Ask children to think about the winter. Which flowers could they see then? Which were the first flowers they spotted this spring? Show them a picture of a snowdrop, ask them to compare it to a flower they can see today. How is it similar or different?

Answers

Children should recognise that there are many different types of flowers. Flowers are different shapes and sizes and they bloom at different times.

Homework suggestions

Make a flower from materials found outside.

Assessment and evidence of learning

Children can:

- begin to identify signs of spring and notice how the space has changed from their last visit
- identify and name some of the flowers they observe
- state that flowers vary in size shape and colour
- compare the observable features of flowers from different plants.

SNAP SCIENCE GET YOUR TEETH INTO IT! 2nd EDITION

Lesson 5: Which birds can we spot?

This lesson should be taught in late spring when there is evidence of birds nesting and hatching. Ideally the bird watching activity will take place over several hours with different groups of children observing at different times.

What children will learn and do

- Children revisit the same outdoor space as in their last seasonal change lesson to observe changes.
- They look for signs of animals, for example: tracks, signs of digging, feeding or nesting.
- They learn that different types of birds can be seen at different times of the year.
- They answer the lesson question: **'Which birds visit our bird feeders?'**

You will need

- to prepare the children to work outside
- cones to mark the outdoor work space
- clipboards

If using the Snap Science Year 1 Pupil Workbook you may not require all of the resource sheets below.

Snap Science Year 1 Pupil Workbook

- pages 14–17

Snap Science Year 1 Digital subscription

- My Seasons Diary
- Resource sheet 1: Bird ID sheet (optional)
- Resource sheet 2: Bird spotter sheet (one for the class to complete)
- Resource sheet 3: Bird ID cards

Make sure you have opened/printed any *Snap* resources you intend to use in this lesson.

National Curriculum

Conceptual knowledge:

- observe changes across the four seasons
- observe and describe weather associated with the seasons and how day length varies
- identify and name a variety of common animals including [fish, amphibians, reptiles,] birds and mammals

Working scientifically:

- observing closely [using simple equipment]
- identifying and classifying
- gathering and recording data to help in answering questions

Scientific enquiry type:

- identifying and classifying

Key vocabulary	
Tier 2 vocabulary:	**Tier 3 vocabulary:**
record, describe	identify, observe
	bird, colour, insect, nest, weather

Health and safety Please refer to CLEAPSS for Health and Safety guidance and ensure that any identified hazards are managed appropriately.

Getting started

This is the fifth of six outdoor lessons across the year. In this session children will look for animals in their space. This lesson builds on work done in Lesson 2 in which children looked for signs of animals sharing their outdoor space. It also builds on Year 1, Module 6: Animals (vertebrates), Lesson 2. This is a two part lesson. In the first part children will look for signs of spring in their space. In the second part, children will do some birdwatching in their space, from a distance. The birdwatching part of the lesson could be done in small groups throughout the day.

As you did last time, begin the session by discussing the weather. Ask children to circle a weather symbol in their My Seasons Diary. Ask children to look back over their diary entries. What was the weather like last time? How has the weather changed? Is it warmer or colder? Wetter or drier? Is it windier?

Discuss spring with the children. What changes can they see happening? Ask children if they notice if there are signs of any new animals in their outside space? Children may observe that there are birds nesting or carrying nesting materials. Explain that when birds are nesting we have to give them space. If we approach nests we can scare the parent birds away which can put the chicks in danger. So it is better to watch from a distance. Ask children if they can see where birds might be building their nests? Children notice that many of the birds in their space build their nests in hard to reach places such as in hedgerows or in tall trees, away from other animals.

Ask children to close their eyes and listen. They may hear birds tweeting and insects buzzing. Ask them to complete the Late spring page in their My Seasons Diary.

Pupil workbook: Complete Activity 1: Today's weather and length of day on page 14 and Activity 2: Signs of spring on page 14.

The task

Part One – Getting to know birds

Tell children that today they are going to answer the lesson question: **'Which birds visit our bird feeders?'**
In this lesson children will observe birds in their space and record the types of bird that they see. In order to help them identify the birds, show children Resource sheet 3: Bird ID cards. Focus on the birds that you know are most likely to be seen in your school grounds, for example blackbird, starling, house sparrow, blue tit, chaffinch, pigeon, robin and magpie.
Each time you show a card, ask children to describe the bird's features. Explain to them that noticing these features will help them to identify which bird they can see. Questions to ask include:
  • What colour are the bird's feathers?
  • What shape is their beak? Cone-shaped like a sparrow's beak? Straight and thin like a robin's beak?
  • What colour are their legs?
  • What shape are their feet? Are they webbed like a gull? Or are they perching feet like a robin?
Ask children to work with a partner and give them a card to look at. Ask them to point to the bird's beak, wings, legs, feet, tail, breast – what colour is each part of the bird's body? What shape is their beak? What shape are their feet? If there is time, children could make their own bird using found natural materials from around their space. Take a photograph of their birds to add to their My Seasons Diary.
Ask children to think about what they have noticed over the last few weeks. Have they spotted any birds on the school bird feeders? What types of birds did they see? Sort through the bird flashcards, allowing children to show you which birds they have seen.

Pupil workbook: Complete Activity 3: Bird spotting on page 15 and Activity 4: Comparing birds on page 16.

Part Two – Birdwatching

The next part of the lesson can take place in small groups over the day, or as a class group. Explain to the children that they are going to make observations of birds that visit the feeding station. To do this the children may need to watch the birds from behind a window, so that they do not disturb them, but even so they will still need to watch quietly!

When birdwatching with your children, ask What type of bird can you see? Where do birds get their food from? As a class, complete Resource sheet 2: Bird spotter sheet. Each group will add their data to the same sheet so that they gather one set of results. Show children how to record their observations on the bird spotter sheet. They should first work out which bird they can see. Then they observe whether they feed from either the bird feeders or on the ground beneath? Can they see what the bird is eating? Are they eating seeds or worms or insects?

Adaptations and support

Some children may need support to identify the birds. They could use Resource sheet 1: Bird ID sheet and simply tick the birds that they see.

Take it further

Ask the children to find out which foods these birds like best. Put out different types of bird food and keep a tally chart of which type of food they feed on most often. You could try black sunflower seeds, pinhead oatmeal, soaked sultanas, mild grated cheese, mealworms, and seed mixtures. (Peanuts should not be put out on the bird feeders in the nesting season as they can be a choking hazard for nestlings.)

Reflect and review

Ask children to look at the data that they collected. What types of birds did they see? Ask children where they saw each type of bird? Which birds did they not see? Ask children to think about what might keep the birds away? Ask them for suggestions how they may encourage more birds into their space.

Reflect on the data you gathered as a class. Sort out the bird ID cards into birds which fed on the feeders and those which fed on the ground. Children may notice that in many cases the ground feeders tend to be bigger birds such as pigeons and blackbirds. This is not entirely true as starlings are great at hanging from bird feeders and small birds such as wrens can often be found feeding on the floor.

Ask children to complete the Bird spotter activity in their My Seasons Diary using the data collected by the whole class.

You could repeat these observations again over the school year. Compare the data each time. Which birds do you see most often?

Pupil workbook: Complete Activity 5: Counting birds on page 17.

> ## Answers
>
> Children may notice that blue tits, sparrows, robins and chaffinches are all more likely to feed on the bird feeders. Blackbirds, wood pigeons, starlings and magpies are all more likely to feed on the ground.
>
> In addition, children may notice that some of the winter birds are no longer around in the springtime. Or they may notice that there are new birds visiting the feeders that they did not see in the winter.

Homework suggestions

Ask children to build their own birds' nest out of found materials. They could use dried grasses, twigs and sticks, and fallen leaves. Ask them to explain where they would put their birds' nests to keep the eggs safe?

SNAP
SCIENCE
GET YOUR TEETH INTO IT!
2nd EDITION

Assessment and evidence of learning

Children can:

- compare the observable features of different bird -- wings, beak, feathers
- collect data in a table of which birds they see at the feeding station
- identify and name some of the birds they observe.

SNAP SCIENCE
GET YOUR TEETH INTO IT!
2nd EDITION

Lesson 6: How has our space changed over the year?

This lesson should be taught in early summer when some plants are producing fruit.

What children will learn and do

- Children revisit the same outdoor space as in their last seasonal change lesson to observe changes.
- They learn that summer is the warmest season of the year, when the sun is highest in the sky, the days are longest and some flowering plants produce fruit.
- They answer the lesson question: **'How has our space changed over the year?'**

You will need

- to prepare the children to work outside
- cones to mark the outdoor work space
- clipboards
- camera (optional)
- heavy book, newspaper and weights (optional)

If using the Snap Science Year 1 Pupil Workbook you may not require all of the resource sheets below.

Snap Science Year 1 Pupil Workbook

- pages 18–21

Snap Science Year 1 Digital subscription

- My Seasons Diary
- Lesson 4 Resource sheet 1: Spring flower ID cards
- Resource sheet 1: Summer flower ID sheet (optional)
- Resource sheet 2: Summer flower ID cards
- Resource sheet 3: Season match sheet
- Snapshot activity 1: Whatever the weather
- Snapshot activity 2: Which season is which?

Make sure you have opened/printed any *Snap* resources you intend to use in this lesson.

National Curriculum

Conceptual knowledge:

- observe changes across the four seasons
- observe and describe weather associated with the seasons and how day length varies

Working scientifically:

- observing closely [using simple equipment]
- identifying and classifying

Scientific enquiry type:

- identifying and classifying

Key vocabulary	
Tier 2 vocabulary: compare, record	**Tier 3 vocabulary:** flower, weather

Health and safety Please refer to CLEAPSS for Health and Safety guidance and ensure that any identified hazards are managed appropriately.

Getting started

This is the final outdoor lesson in this module. As you did last time, begin the session by discussing the weather. Ask children to circle a weather symbol in their My Seasons Diary. Ask children to look back over their diary entries. What was the weather like last time? How has the weather changed?

Ask children what season it is. Confirm that it is summer. What changes can they see happening? Ask children if they notice if there are signs of any new animals in their outside space? Children may observe that it has got hotter. Explain that summer is the warmest season of the year, when the sun is highest in the sky in the summer and the days are longest. Ask children to complete the My summer visit page in their My Seasons Diary.

Show children Lesson 4 Resource sheet 1: Spring flower ID cards. Ask children if they can see those flowers now? Children will notice that those plants are no longer in flower. Then show children Resource sheet 2: Summer flower ID cards. Talk about the colour and shape of each flower. Ask children to look in the grass. Can they see any of these flowers?

Tell children that today they are going to answer the lesson question: **'How has our space changed over the year?'**

Pupil workbook: Complete Activity 1: Today's weather and length of day on page 18 and Activity 2: Signs of summer on page 18.

The task

Ask children to complete the Summer flower spotter in their My Seasons Diary. Choose a flower and show them how to record that flower on the grid by ticking in the correct colour square. Children then complete the sheet with all the flowers they can find. Ask them to compare their spring and summer flower spotter sheets. How are the colours the same or different?

Ask children to look back through their My Season Diary with a friend. Ask them to find something that they spotted in the autumn, winter, spring and summer. Look at the trees in your space. How have they changed over the year? For example, the deciduous tree lost its leaves in the winter while the evergreen tree shed its leaves over the year. Use these ideas to complete the final page in their My Season Diary and answer the lesson question: **'How has our space changed over the year?'**

Pupil workbook: Complete Activity 3: Flower colours in summer on page 19, Activity 4: Changes in the year on page 20 and Activity 5: Weather and length of day on page 21.

Adaptations and support

Children could take photographs of different flowers that they see and use these to make a collage of summer flowers. Or they could use Resource sheet 1: Summer flower ID sheet and tick the flowers that they see.

Take it further

Tell children to make a collection of pressed flowers. Collect one of each flower that they see. Open a book and line it with a sheet of dry newspaper. Place the flowers on the page. Close the book and weigh it down. Store in a warm, dry place and check on the flower specimens daily. Press the flowers until they are dry. Use the pressed flowers to make new flower ID cards.

Reflect and review

Give pairs of children Resource sheet 3: Season match sheet. Can they match up the natural event to the season? Ask children to reflect on their outdoor lessons this year. Which was their favourite season and why?

Pupil workbook: Complete Activity 6: Season match on page 21.

Answers

Spring – trees blossom

Summer – fruit

Autumn – leaves change colour

Winter – trees lose their leaves

Homework suggestions

Make a simple butterfly feeder. You will need an old jar lid. Place on it small pieces of over-ripe fruit. Place it outside in a sheltered but sunny spot for example, on your balcony or in your garden on a warm day. Allow some time for it to attract butterflies. Draw a picture of any butterflies or other insects that come and feed.

Assessment and evidence of learning

Children can:

- compare the flowers from different seasons
- describe how their space changed over the year
- match natural events to each season.

If you are unsure if a child knows the weather in different seasons you can use the Snapshot: Whatever the weather to check understanding and develop their learning.

If you are unsure if a child knows what you observe in each season you can use the Snapshot: Which season is which? to check understanding and develop their learning.

Module 2: Human body and senses

Lesson 1: Is everyone's body the same?

What children will learn and do

- Children learn that humans are mammals.
- They label the names of the basic parts of the human body.
- They learn that eyes enable us to see and that sight is the sense that enables us to see.
- They answer the lesson question: **'Is everyone's body the same?'**

In this lesson, children are building knowledge of variation and understanding of difference within an age-appropriate context. These differences should be handled with sensitivity.

You will need

- large open space such as hall or playground
- lengths of lining/backing paper and pens
- chalk
- sticky notes and pencils
- blindfolds (optional)

Snap Science Year 1 Pupil Workbook

- pages 22–24

Snap Science Year 1 Digital subscription

- Snapshot activity 1: Body parts

Make sure you have opened/printed any *Snap* resources you intend to use in this lesson.

National Curriculum

Conceptual knowledge:

- identify, name, draw and label basic parts of the human body and say which part of the body is associated with each sense

Working scientifically:

- asking simple questions and recognising that they can be answered in different ways

Key vocabulary	
Tier 2:	Tier 3:
	group, diagram identify
	brain, mammal, sense, sight, torso

Health and safety Please refer to CLEAPSS for Health and Safety guidance and ensure that any identified hazards are managed appropriately.

Getting started

Talk with the children about the human body and parts they can identify and name. Ask them to talk to each other and by pointing to parts of their own body, to name them. During this activity, listen carefully for children's questions, making note of them to come back to later in this lesson or the rest of the module as appropriate.

Collect names for body parts centrally as a class after this activity with particular focus on parts of their body such as arm, leg, head, chest, neck, hand, fingers, feet and toes. Ensure the word torso is used and understood if not offered. Children may offer other visible parts such as eyes, ears or hair, collect these too.

If internal organs or bones are named, collect these, but in a separate list. Value these contributions but make it clear that this is not essential knowledge for the whole class in this lesson. Use this as a chance to pick up on any misconceptions at this stage and ensure the words you collect are in a space that the children can access for reference later.

Tell children that humans are animals and they are mammals. That is one of the groups that scientists who work with animals group and organise animals into. They will learn more about this in Module 5 (Animals).

Tell them that they are going to be answering the lesson question: **'Is everyone's body the same?'** in today's lesson. Now tell them they will be drawing and labelling their own life size diagram of their body parts. Working in pairs:

- one of them lies down and is drawn around on a length of lining paper with pens
- or one of them lies down and is drawn around on the playground with chalks
- or one of them is labelled with sticky notes.

While the children are doing this, encourage them to notice things that are the same and things that are different about each other's bodies. They might suggest hair or eye colour, shoe size or height. Ensure these are all handled sensitively and appropriately for your class to ensure every child feels safe to share.

Once again, review any misconceptions at this stage, correcting as appropriate or noting to address later.

Pupil workbook: Complete Activity 1: Labelling body parts on page 22.

The task

Focus on the faces of the large, labelled diagrams they have done in pairs and draw their attention to the eyes, nose, ears and mouth. If they are not already labelled, tell them to do that now.

Tell children that in this module they are going to be studying their senses and how they help them to tell what is happening in the world around them. Tell them these are called: sight, touch, hearing, smell and taste and that today, they will look at sight in more detail.

Ask them to talk to their partner about this question: How can we see? Collect all responses, no matter how correct at this stage.

Tell them we see with our eyes which send messages to our brain which helps us to make sense of the world around us.

Tell them to play 'I spy with my little eye …' with their partner, supporting them to choose things they can see in the room by modelling it first. Now play again but this time ask them to close their eyes. Don't leave it too long before noting it is too difficult to see without our eyes.

Play various games in the open space to explore what happens if they can't see, for example use blindfolds and guide a partner around the space or give verbal instructions to a partner to guide them from one place to another. Note how difficult this is without our eyes to see.

Ask the class to reflect on how their eyes help them to stay safe, move around and notice what is happening around them. Tell them that eyes send messages to the brain and it is the brain that helps us to understand what we are seeing. Without our eyes to send the messages, our brains have to rely on other senses, such as touch, to understand what is around us. Touch will be explored in the next lesson.

Pupil workbook: Complete Activity 2: The sense of sight on page 23.

Adaptations and support

Provide ready-made labels of body part names for any children unable to write them when drawing the bodies. Provide appropriate support for any children with visual impairment when playing 'I spy'.

Take it further

Connect with a charity that supports people with sight impairment such as RNIB. They are often happy to come into school with guide dogs and support the children's awareness of adaptations to the environment needed.

Draw sensitively on any first-hand experiences within the class or school community of sight impairment to support the understanding of how we see and what happens when we can't.

Reflect and review

Remind children of the lesson question they are answering today: **'Is everyone's body the same?'**

Tell them to talk to a partner about ways human bodies are the same. Expect age-appropriate responses that reflect the lesson content such as 'we all have two legs' or 'we all have toes'.

Tell them to talk to a partner about ways human bodies are different. Expect age-appropriate responses that reflect the lesson content such as 'I'm taller than you' or 'Some of us have brown hair like mine and some don't'.

Tell them to talk to a partner about things they could not see if they had their eyes shut. Expect responses that are appropriate to the question and the lesson so far.

Pupil workbook: Complete Activity 3: Are all bodies the same? on page 24.

Answers

All humans are animals. All humans are mammals. Human bodies are generally the same, two arms, two legs etc. Humans vary in size, skin, hair and eye colour, shoe size, height, fingerprint and many other aspects.

Homework suggestions

Practise naming parts of the body by playing games like 'Simon Says' at home.

Assessment and evidence of learning

Children can:

- state that humans are animals
- state that humans are mammals
- name at least ten body parts
- know some differences between human bodies such as hair colour, height or hand span
- know some similarities between human bodies such as two arms and two legs.

If you are unsure if a child can identify, name, draw and label basic parts of the human body you can use Snapshot activity 1: Body parts to check understanding and develop the learning.

Children can:

- state that we see things with our eyes.

SNAP SCIENCE
GET YOUR TEETH INTO IT!
2nd EDITION

Lesson 2: How can we explore the world using our sense of touch?

What children will learn and do

- Children revisit naming and identifying the basic parts of the body.
- They learn that we can use any part of our skin to feel things and that this is our sense of touch.
- They explore their sense of touch using different body parts.
- They answer the lesson question: **'How can we explore the world using our sense of touch?'**

You will need

- three stations of touch activity – enough for a third of the class to be exploring each in pairs at any one time
- feely feet trays using deep trays or kitchen bowl type containers with different materials. Examples include: polystyrene shapes, lengths of bubble wrap, crumpled paper, feathers, fine gravel, cornflakes, wet sand or jelly mix. Blindfolds (for example jumpers) and tray covers will be helpful too
- feely bags – drawstring bags with familiar objects such as a large seashell or large pine cone, a hairbrush, a shoe, a soft toy, a torch, a toy truck, an orange, pineapple or cabbage
- hot and cold – a selection of warm and cold everyday items such as microwaveable warmers and some everyday objects that have been placed in the fridge
- an electronic way to record children speaking, such as sound buttons or a voice app. How many of these needed will depend on preferred recording methods

If using the Snap Science Year 1 Pupil Workbook you may not require all of the resource sheets below.

Snap Science Year 1 Pupil Workbook

- pages 25–27

Snap Science Year 1 Digital subscription

- Video 1: A baby's sense of touch
- Resource sheet 1: Feely feet
- Resource sheet 2: Feely bags
- Resource sheet 3: Comparing temperature by touch

Make sure you have opened/printed any *Snap* resources you intend to use in this lesson.

National Curriculum

Conceptual knowledge:

- identify, name, draw and label basic parts of the human body and say which part of the body is associated with each sense

Working scientifically:

- observing closely, using simple equipment

Key vocabulary	
Tier 2 vocabulary:	**Tier 3 vocabulary:**
texture	identify
	brain, sense, touch

Health and safety Please refer to CLEAPSS for Health and Safety guidance and ensure that any identified hazards are managed appropriately.

Getting started

Revisit naming and identifying basic parts of the human body from Lesson 1 by playing a game of 'Simon Says'. Notice if children are not confident with naming particular body part names or are checking with a classmate before touching them and address this at a suitable time.

Tell them we are going to be finding out about another sense today by answering the lesson question: **'How can we explore the world using our sense of touch?'**

Show Video 1: A baby's sense of touch, which shows a baby touching things as a form of discovery. After watching the video, ask children to talk to a partner about: How does the baby find out about the world around them? What parts of the body do they use to touch things? How do they find out more about objects and people? What parts of our bodies do we use to feel our world? What can we find out by touching something?

Tell them that the skin is the largest single part of our bodies and that it sends messages to the brain about what we can feel so we can make sense of what we feel. It can help to keep us safe from harm such as burning or being squashed.

Pupil workbook: Complete Activity 1: Exploring the world on page 25.

The task

Set up three stations around the space the lesson is in, allowing for all children to explore all three touch stations during the lesson. Recording strategies will vary depending on how independent the children are with this.

Feely feet touch station: Working in pairs, children wear blindfolds and use their feet alone to help them to describe and compare textures of the contents of the covered feely feet trays. A sound recorder along with the words on Resource sheet 1: Feely feet will help them to verbalise how each of the materials felt.
Feely bag touch station: Working in pairs, children use their hands and sense of touch to help them describe, identify and name objects hidden in feely bags. Each bag contains a hidden object. They should explore at least six objects and describe how each object feels using Resource sheet 2: Feely bags.

Hot and cold touch station: Working in pairs, children use their sense of touch to feel different temperatures and how this is different on different parts of their body. Placing a range of cool and warm objects on their skin for a few seconds, they test them on different parts of their body including wrist, cheek, forehead and fingertip. Use Resource sheet 3: Comparing temperature by touch to record temperature difference on a sliding scale.

Pupil workbook: Complete Activity 2: Feely feet on page 25, Activity 3: Feely bags on page 26 and Activity 4: Warm and cold on page 27.

Adaptations and support

Children could use a sound recorder to record their observations at the feely bag and feel feet stations. At the hot and cold touch station sorting hoops could be used instead of the recording sheet, or the sliding scale with adult support.

Take it further

Some children may consider how people with another sensory impairment such as lack of sight might rely on touch to help them explore the world around them.

Remind children of how they covered their eyes in the previous lesson and that meant they had to listen to their partner or reach out to touch to find their way around safely.

Reflect and review

Remind children the lesson question they are learning about today is: **'How can we explore the world using touch?'**

Ask them to help you to make a list of body parts (covered with skin) they have used to explore the sense of touch today.

Talk to them about parts of their body that were best at noticing hot and cold or the texture or hardness of something? For example, feet or fingers for texture? Cheek or forehead for temperature?

Establish that we use our sense of touch to find out about the world around us and that our whole bodies help us to feel things that we come in contact with. We do this with our skin that covers our whole bodies.

Answers

We use our skin to touch and feel things and make sense of the world around us. This is particularly important when it comes to keeping us safe from extremes of temperature.

Any body part covered in skin can be used for touch. Some are more sensitive to temperature than others. For example, the most sensitive heat receptors are found on elbows, nose, and fingertips. Cold receptors are found on the chest, chin, nose, finger, and the upper lip. The nose has hot and cold heat receptors.

Homework suggestions

Children could show a grown-up at home how objects can feel different using different body parts. A coat for example or a soft toy might feel different with your cheek, your elbow or the sole of your foot.

Assessment and evidence of learning

Children can:
- describe observations using sensory and context-specific vocabulary (roughness, temperature, texture etc.)
- state that we feel things with touch and that this is using our skin which covers our whole bodies.

Lesson 3: What can we hear?

What children will learn and do

- Children revisit naming and identifying the basic parts of the body.
- They learn that our ears enable us to hear and that this is our sense of hearing.
- They explore their sense of hearing on a sound walk and sort them into loud and quiet sounds.
- They answer the lesson question: **'What can we hear?'**

You will need

- two or three large dice with each side labelled with a different basic body part (arm, leg, head, torso etc.)
- to take the class on a sound walk around the school buildings and grounds. This can be as a whole class or in small groups as required
- paper, pencils and clipboards per child for the sound walk
- pack of sticky notes
- two or three sorting hoops

Note that in this lesson children need to walk around the school grounds listening for different sounds.

Snap Science Year 1 Pupil Workbook

- pages 28–29

Snap Science Year 1 Digital subscription

- Slideshow 1: What's my sound?

Make sure you have opened/printed any *Snap* resources you intend to use in this lesson

National Curriculum

Conceptual knowledge:

- identify, name, draw and label basic parts of the human body and say which part of the body is associated with each sense

Working scientifically:

- identifying and classifying

Scientific enquiry type:

- identifying and classifying

Key vocabulary	
Tier 2 vocabulary:	**Tier 3 vocabulary:**
	group, identify
	brain, hearing, sense, sight, touch

Health and safety Please refer to CLEAPSS for Health and Safety guidance and ensure that any identified hazards are managed appropriately.

Getting started

Revisit naming and identifying basic parts of the human body from Lesson 1 by playing a dice game. Roll the pre-prepared dice all at once and shout out the body parts on display. Can children touch both parts at the same time (for example head and feet)? Notice if children are becoming more confident today with naming particular body part names. Note any children who remain challenged by this and address it at a suitable time.

Ask children to recall the senses they have already learned about in the first two lessons of the module. Ensure they can remember sight and touch and that in both cases, messages are sent to the brain to help us to make sense of the world around us.

Tell them they are going to find out about another sense today by answering the lesson question: **'What can we hear?'**

Start by asking children what they think their ears are for and what they help us to do. Tell them to complete this sentence to a partner 'I use my ears to...' Model as required.

Play the sounds in Slideshow 1: What's my sound? one at a time and model how to identify the sound with questions such as: Is it a loud sound? Is it a quiet sound? Does it remind you of anything? Have you heard the sound before? Where might we hear this sound? What is making the sound?

Pupil workbook: Complete Activity 1: Everyday sounds on page 28.

The task

Tell the children they are going on a sound walk around school and are going to be gathering a list of sounds they hear on their way.

Provide each child with paper, pencils and clipboards and discuss possible recording methods such as a list, drawings or a map. How they record is not important, recording the sounds is.

When complete, ask children to look at their record of sounds and count how many they heard. Ask them some questions about their sounds and share their responses together for example: how many sounds were loud? How many were quiet? Where were you when you heard the most sounds? Where were there the fewest sounds? How far away was the sound being made? Were the nearest sounds the loudest?

Ask children to write what made one sound from their list, perhaps their favourite, on a sticky note each and gather them in a shared space where you can make some sliding scales at either end of the room.

Ask more questions but this time they answer about the one sound on their sticky note and move around the room to show their answer for example: Was your sound loud? If so, stand over this side of the room. Can you find someone who has the same sound as you? Can you find someone whose sound was from a different part of school to you?

Then, prompt children to suggest different ways of grouping the sounds they have on their sticky notes, for example, sounds made by nature, sounds made by mechanical objects for example, sounds that are musical and those that are not. Model as required.

Pupil workbook: Complete Activity 2: Sound walk on page 29.

Adaptations and support

Some children may draw rather than write the names of what made the sounds they observed.

Take it further

Some children may explore means of communication used by people with a hearing impairment. They could learn some British Sign Language signs for hello, please, thank you or goodbye.

Reflect and review

Remind children of the lesson question: **'What can we hear?'**

Tell them to talk to a partner about all the sounds they have heard today. Expect responses appropriate to the lesson context.

Support the children to explore ways of making sounds louder, such as cupping their hand around their ear, or quieter, by covering one or both ears. This could be when you are playing a musical instrument or simply speaking aloud to them.

Establish that we use our hearing senses to make sense of the world around us. We do this by using our ears to hear.

SNAP SCIENCE
GET YOUR TEETH INTO IT!
2nd EDITION

Answers

We use our ears to hear sounds and to make sense of the world around us.

Homework suggestions

Ask children to answer: How many different sounds can you hear on your way home tonight? What sounds do you hear on the way to school tomorrow morning? Are any of these sounds the same?

Assessment and evidence of learning

Children can:

- state that we hear things with our ears
- observe differences between sounds and identify what made the different sounds.

SNAP SCIENCE
GET YOUR TEETH INTO IT!
2nd EDITION

Lesson 4: What smells do we like and dislike?

What children will learn and do

- Children revisit naming and identifying the basic parts of the body.
- They learn that our nose enables us to smell and is our fourth sense.
- They explore which smells they like and dislike and how this compares to their classmates.
- They answer the lesson question: **'What smells do we like and dislike?'**

You will need

- each group of four children will need at least six clearly numbered 'smelly pots'. These could be made from repurposed pots, boxes or jars with holes in the lids, containers with pieces of gauze held over the tops using elastic bands, or paper bags sealed with an elastic band
- different 'smelly objects' making use of food scraps and everyday objects where possible. Examples include, cheese and onion crisp packet, brown sauce, toffee, apple core, lemon zest, rubber bands, pencil shavings, curry powder, strong cheese, orange peel, onion peel, basil leaves, garlic peelings, ginger scraps, rosemary leaves, lavender seeds, cloves, vinegar, modelling clay, soap shavings, yeast extract spread, tomato puree, toothpaste and chocolate
- three or four of the 'smelly objects' to duplicate and have uncovered for the 'getting started' part of the lesson

If using the Snap Science Year 1 Pupil Workbook you may not require the resource sheet below.

Snap Science Year 1 Pupil Workbook

- pages 30–31

Snap Science Year 1 Digital subscription

- Resource sheet 1: Which smells do we like … and which do we dislike?

Make sure you have opened/printed any *Snap* resources you intend to use in this lesson.

National Curriculum

Conceptual knowledge:

- identify, name, draw and label basic parts of the human body and say which part of the body is associated with each sense

Working scientifically:

- gathering and recording data to help in answering questions

Key vocabulary	
Tier 2 vocabulary:	**Tier 3 vocabulary:** identify, pattern brain, hearing, sense, sight, smell, touch

Health and safety Please refer to CLEAPSS for Health and Safety guidance and ensure that any identified hazards are managed appropriately.

Getting started

Start by revisiting the names of the basic parts of the human body by singing a song such as 'heads-shoulders-knees-and-toes', inserting any key words that you've noticed some children do not yet remember such as torso or elbow.

Remind children they have been learning about human senses and help them to recall sight, touch and hearing that they have found out about so far. Tell them today, they will be learning about a fourth sense – smell and answering the lesson question: **'Which smells do we like and dislike?'**

Pass the uncovered 'smelly objects' around the class, naming them as you do, so all the children get to smell each one. Model how to sniff each item carefully and ask them which parts of their body they are using to smell with. Expect them to say their nose and they might also say their brain by making connections to how the other senses they have learnt about work.

Once all the objects have been smelt, organise a simple voting system to work out which smells the class liked and which ones they didn't. Help them to notice that there will be differences and personal preferences between them.

Tell children that, like all the other senses they have explored so far, the nose sends messages to the brain to help us make sense of what we have smelt.

Pupil workbook: Complete Activity 1: What body parts do you know now? on page 30.

The task

Children work in small groups (suggest four) to smell at least six objects using one copy of Resource sheet 1: Which smells do we like … and which do we dislike? per group to record their smell preferences.

Tell them to use their completed table to feed back to the rest of the class which smell was liked the most in their group and which one was liked the least.

As a class, establish if these likes and dislikes were the same across the class and if certain smells were more popular than others. Is there a pattern?

Make the point that we all have different likes and dislikes – and that is fine. Often a smell reminds us of something we like or enjoy and that can be why we like the smell when we sniff it again.

Although not the focus, the children may wish to know what the smells were, so ensure you have a list of what was in each numbered pot for sharing if required.

Pupil workbook: Complete Activity 2: Which smells do we like and dislike? on page 31.

Adaptations and support

Support children with recording smell preferences where required.

Take it further

Some children may explore how a reduced sense of smell might affect how much you like or dislike a smell. Children could try smelling the pots again whilst holding their nose and see if they still like and dislike the same smells.

Reflect and review

Remind children of the lesson question: **What smells do we like and dislike?**

Ask them to tell you which parts of their bodies they use to smell and expect them to name the nose. some children may mention the brain too. as a response.

Ask them if they noticed any pattern in the smells that most children liked and any pattern in the smells most children didn't like.

Answers

Each person's response to smells may be different. Our innate response to a smell is often connected to a personal memory or experience from when we first smelt it. One person may love the smell of baking bread or freshly mown grass whilst others dislike it intensely.

SNAP SCIENCE
GET YOUR TEETH INTO IT!
2nd EDITION

Homework suggestions

Ask children to make some smelly pots at home for family members to guess the smell.

Ask people at home what their favourite smells are – are they the same as yours? What about the ones they dislike? Are they the same too?

Assessment and evidence of learning

Children can:
- state that we smell things with our noses
- record their observations in a table.

Lesson 5: What differences can our tongues taste?

What children will learn and do

- Children revisit naming and identifying the basic parts of the body.
- They learn that our tongues, along with noses and eyes, help us taste food and drink.
- They explore their sense of taste and sort different foods into sweet and sour.
- They answer the lesson question: **'What differences can our tongues taste?'**

You will need

- small samples of sour and sweet foodstuffs to taste test, for example: orange segments, honey, syrup, vinegar, orange squash, natural yoghurt, jam, soy sauce, mint sweet, dark chocolate, dried fruit, pickled gherkin
- lemon juice and sugar (plus their packaging) as these will be used by all in the tasks
- one reusable teaspoon per child

Note: avoid food waste where possible by using foods already available. The children will only be tasting very tiny amounts each time so limit volume

If using the Snap Science Year 1 Pupil Workbook you may not require the resource sheet below.

Snap Science Year 1 Pupil Workbook

- pages 32–33

Snap Science Year 1 Digital subscription

- Resource sheet 1: Taste testing
- Snapshot activity 1: Body parts and senses

Make sure you have opened/printed any *Snap* resources you intend to use in this lesson.

National Curriculum

Conceptual knowledge:

- identify, name, draw and label basic parts of the human body and say which part of the body is associated with each sense

Working scientifically:

- identifying and classifying

Key vocabulary	
Tier 2 vocabulary:	Tier 3 vocabulary: group, identify, rank brain, hearing, sense, sight, smell, taste, touch

Health and safety Please refer to CLEAPSS for Health and Safety guidance and ensure that any identified hazards are managed appropriately.

Ensure that children realise that they should not taste anything that they encounter during a science lesson, with one exception, which is when they carry out a taste test under teacher supervision.

Be aware of food allergies in your class before this lesson and provide samples accordingly.

Getting started

Revisit identifying and naming the basic parts of the human body once more to ensure these are secure using a method of the children's choice from the previous lessons (Simon Says, Heads-shoulders-knees and toes, dice game, etc.).

Remind children they have been learning about the human body's senses and which parts of the body are associated with each one. Recall each one in turn ensuring children can recall the body parts correctly. Expect eyes + brain = sight, skin + brain = touch, ears + brain = hearing, nose + brain = smell.

Tell them today they will be finding out about the fifth and final sense of taste. Ask them to think about what body parts they think help them taste. Collect any and all responses in a list without responding to them at this point and return to them later in the lesson.

Ask children to recall something they tasted (food or drink) recently that they liked and share it. Repeat with something they recently tasted that they didn't like.

Pupil workbook: Complete Activity 1: How do we sense things? on page 32.

The task

Children will work alone, but alongside classmates, to taste foodstuffs and rank how they taste on a sour to sweet scale. Support their understanding of this by giving everyone a couple of drops of lemon juice on their spoons to try followed by a few grains of sugar.

Use Resource sheet 1: Taste testing and model how to record these first two entries on the sliding scale.

Then, allow children to choose things from the selection you have provided to taste at least four more foodstuffs and rank on the sour to sweet scale. More can be tried if time allows. Encourage children to draw their own extra table of results if required.

Bring the class together with their taste test results and place the lemon juice at one side of the room and sugar at the other, explaining to the class that this is the same way of ranking the tastes as they have done on their tables.

Choose several of the foodstuffs provided and ask children to stand on the scale where they thought it was in terms of sour to sweet. Support them to notice if their opinion was different to their classmates. Reassure them that this is okay as taste is a personal preference, there are no right or wrong answers.

Pupil workbook: Complete Activity 2: Taste testing on page 33.

Adaptations and support

Support children to taste things appropriately to their personal preferences and be aware of any sensory needs in this lesson.

Take it further

Some children may explore other tastes, such as spicy, salty and bitter.

Reflect and review

Remind the children of the lesson question: **'What differences can our tongues taste?'**

Ask them to tell a partner something sour they have tasted today and something sweet. Expect responses that match their earlier views.

Ask them to tell a partner what parts of their body they use to taste. Expect tongue and brain. Some children may also mention eyes and nose alongside tongue.

Establish that we use our sense of taste to make sense of the world around us. We do this by using our tongues.

Answers

Our tongues, along with noses and eyes, help us to taste things.

Taste is personal preference, much like smell, but uses multiple senses to make decisions about like and dislike.

Sour and sweet are only two things our tongues can taste. Salty, bitter and spicy are examples of others – this lesson focuses on just these two.

Homework suggestions

Ask children to report back in the classroom the next morning about any food they ate at home that was sour and anything that was sweet. Add it to the class scale.

Assessment and evidence of learning

Children can:

- state that we taste things with our tongues
- state that we also use our senses of sight and smell (with eyes and noses) to decide if we like something or not
- rank food and drinks into groups by how sweet or sound they taste.

If you are unsure if a child can identify, name, draw and label basic parts of the human body associated with each sense, you can use Snapshot activity 1: Body parts and senses to check understanding and develop the learning.

Module 3: Naming and describing materials

Lesson 1: What material is this? Part 1

What children will learn and do

- Children learn that everything around us is made of materials.
- They learn that some materials are natural materials, and we use them without modifying them.
- They learn that some materials are manufactured materials, natural materials that have been made into another material.
- They use their senses to explore the properties of wood, metal and plastic.
- They group objects by the type of material they are made of.
- They answer the lesson question: **'What material is this?'**

You will need

- wood offcuts: small pieces of planking, blocks, dowelling
- small sections of tree branches/twigs
- artefacts and toys made only from wood
- metal samples or small ingots of metal
- objects and toys made only from metal
- corrugated and other sheet plastic to show basic plastic
- objects and toys made only from plastic
- sorting hoops with labels 'wood', 'metal' and 'plastic'
- images of common objects made of wood, metal or plastic (e.g. pages from a brochure or catalogue)

Snap Science Year 1 Pupil Workbook

- pages 34–36

National Curriculum

Conceptual knowledge:

- identify and name a variety of everyday materials, including wood, plastic, [glass], metal, [water and rock]

Working scientifically:

- observing closely, [using simple equipment]

Scientific enquiry type:

- identifying and classifying

Key vocabulary	
Tier 2 vocabulary:	**Tier 3 vocabulary:**
describe, different, similar, sort	observe
Descriptive language such as, flexible/rigid, rough/smooth, shiny/dull, soft/hard	manufactured, material, natural, property
Comparative language such as, bigger/smaller, rougher/smoother, softer/harder	

Health and safety Please refer to CLEAPSS for Health and Safety guidance and ensure that any identified hazards are managed appropriately.

Getting started

Show children different samples of wood, including wood offcuts and small sections of branches. Pass some of these around the class and ask them what the samples are made from. Ask them if they know the name of this material and where it comes from. Introduce the term natural to the children. Explain that wood is a type of material that is natural, as it grows in trees. Ask them if they know of anything else which has been made of wood. This might be a favourite toy from home or something around the classroom. Show children three wooden objects (ensure there are no parts that are not made of wood). Ask them what they are made of and how they are different from the offcuts. Ensure that they recognise that the wooden objects are made of wood that has been shaped for a purpose. Put all the wooden items in a large hoop labelled 'wood'. Tell them that this group of items all have something in common: they are made of wood.

Repeat with the metal samples and three metal objects and place them in a hoop labelled 'metal'. How are they different from the wooden ones? Focus on observable properties such as texture, colour, weight and temperature to the touch. Introduce the word property as the word we use to say what a material is like.

Repeat again with the corrugated plastic sheet and three plastic objects, and place in a hoop labelled 'plastic'. Introduce the term manufactured to the children in simple terms. Explain that metal and plastic materials are manufactured materials because they have been made by changing a natural material.

Tell children that today's lesson question is: **'What material is this?'** They will use their observation skills to help them identify different materials around the classroom. Remind them that to make an observation they can use different senses; their eyes to see what a material looks like, but also their sense of touch and perhaps even their sense of hearing.

Pupil workbook: Complete Activity 1: Wood, metal or plastic? on page 34 and Activity 2: Comparing objects on page 35.

The task

Divide children into three groups. Ask each group to find as many examples as they can of either wood, metal or plastic in the classroom, and label them with sticky notes. Take photographs of parts of the classroom where there are examples of several different materials in close proximity.

Adaptations and support

Give children requiring more focused support a large bag of objects made from the three materials to sort. It is important that individual objects are made from only one of the materials. For example, a wooden toy must have no metal or plastic components. Ask children to sort the objects, using the hoops, into the three categories of wood, metal and plastic. Any they are not sure about should be left outside the hoops. Take a photograph of the completed hoops.

Take it further

Children can identify and list other objects made of these three materials which are not found in the classroom. Provide a selection of pictures and catalogue pages with examples of objects made from the three materials to focus this task.

Reflect and review

Remind children of today's lesson question: **'What material is this?'**

Select some of the objects labelled by the children as made from either wood, metal or plastic. Ensure that the objects you choose include contrasting objects made of the same material.

Ask children what they notice about the objects. Ask how are they similar and how are they different? Encourage them to describe the properties of the objects.

Ask children how they used their science skill of observation to sort the object into three groups, according to the material they are made from. Remind them that they used their sense of sight to find the objects and sense of touch to help them identify the properties of the different materials used to make the objects.

Select some objects from around the classroom and ask children to name the material each is made of and describe their properties, checking that they are using appropriate descriptive and comparative language correctly as they do so. Provide several 'new' objects made of two different materials and use these to test out children's identification skills. Can they name the two materials? Can they suggest why different materials might be used for different parts of the object?

Remind children of the terms mentioned in the 'Getting started' part of the lesson, 'natural' and 'manufactured'. Can anyone remember what those words mean? Ask children: Which of the materials we have observed today is a natural material? Which is a manufactured material?

Remind children once more of the lesson question: **'What material is this?'** and consider responses from them that recognise the many differences, including whether the materials are natural or manufactured in origin.

Pupil workbook: Complete Activity 3: Natural or manufactured? on page 36.

Answers

Children should identify and group objects made of the same material, while recognising that materials of the same type can have very different properties e.g. these objects are all made of plastic: the plastic bag is shiny and flexible, the plastic ruler is shiny and rigid.

Children name wood as a natural material that grows in the form of trees. They name metal and plastic as manufactured materials because they have been made by changing a natural material.

Homework suggestions

Challenge children to find a toy or another object made of each of the three materials that feature in this lesson. They might share what they find by sketching the objects, taking a photograph of them, or bringing one or more of the objects into school.

Assessment and evidence of learning

Children can:

- identify wood, metal and plastic in a range of objects
- sort objects made of these materials into groups and describe their physical properties
- give examples of other objects made from wood, metal and plastic, and distinguish the object from the material(s) from which it is made
- use the words 'wood', 'metal' and 'plastic' correctly when talking about objects and the materials they are made from
- use appropriate vocabulary to describe observations and make comparisons of materials and objects
- recognise wood as a natural material and metal and plastic as manufactured materials.

Lesson 2: What material is this? Part 2

What children will learn and do

- Children use their senses to explore the properties of glass, water and rock.
- They group objects by the type of material they are made from.
- They learn that materials should be used carefully and can often be reused or recycled.
- They answer the lesson question: **'What material is this?'**

You will need

- objects made of glass
- bricks
- rock samples
- water and cups
- paper and drawing equipment
- pictures of the four materials (from magazines)
- sorting hoops
- labels/sticky notes
- magnifiers

If using the Snap Science Year 1 Pupil Workbook you may not require all of the resource sheets below.

Snap Science Year 1 Pupil Workbook

- pages 37–39

Snap Science Year 1 Digital subscription

- Resource sheet 1: Water or glass?
- Resource sheet 2: Rocks or bricks?
- Resource sheet 3: Wood, plastic or metal?
- Video 1: Lots of water
- Slideshow 1: Naturally occurring rocks

Make sure you have opened/printed any *Snap* resources you intend to use in this lesson.

National Curriculum

Conceptual knowledge:

- identify and name a variety of everyday materials, including [wood, plastic], glass, [metal], water and rock

Working scientifically:

- observing closely, using simple equipment

Scientific enquiry type:

- identifying classifying

Key vocabulary	
Tier 2 vocabulary:	**Tier 3 vocabulary:**
different, describe, record, similar, sort	group, magnifier
Adjectives to describe children's sensory explorations of materials' physical properties	manufactured, material, natural, observe, property, recycle, transparent

Health and safety Please refer to CLEAPSS for Health and Safety guidance and ensure that any identified hazards are managed appropriately.

Getting started

Remind children that the world is full of many different materials. Some are natural and some are manufactured. Encourage them to think back to the last lesson. Ask: What were the names of the materials we observed? Were they natural or manufactured?

Tell them that it is important that we are very careful how we use all materials and introduce the terms reuse and recycle. Assuming that waste in school is collected, sorted and recycled in some way, draw children's attention to what happens and why. Encourage children to recognise the importance of not wasting materials and recycling materials to be used again whenever possible.

Introduce the next selection of materials.

Show children examples of objects made from glass. Ask: Do you know what material these objects are made from? Why do you think they are not being passed around? Can you think of words to describe glass? Answers should focus on properties that can be observed using the sense of sight, such as colour and transparency.

Ask them if they can name anything else made of glass in the classroom and then carefully label the objects with a sticky note. Place the glass objects in a labelled hoop. Ask: What properties do the glass objects have in common? Can you think of any other objects made from glass? Tell them that glass is a manufactured material, made from sand and other materials.

Show children naturally occurring rocks using Slideshow 1: Naturally occurring rocks, which includes images of rock samples and pictures of rocky environments. Pass rock samples around the class and ask them if they know what they are. Tell the children that the scientific name is 'rocks', not 'stones'. What words describe the rocks? Place the samples in a labelled hoop. What properties do these rocks have in common? Tell them that rocks are natural materials.

Show children examples of bricks, if possible small and light enough for children to handle. Pass them around and ask if they know what they are. Place the bricks in a labelled hoop. Ask: Can you think of any words to describe brick? What are bricks used for? Where might we see them? What properties do these bricks have in common? Tell them that brick is a manufactured material, made from clay (a type of rock) and other materials.

Show children Video 1: Lots of water, which shows water, another natural material, in different places. Pour water from a jug into transparent beakers. Ask: What is this called? What words can you think of to describe water? How is it different from the other three materials? Does it have any similarities? Place the beakers of water in a labelled hoop.

Tell children that today's lesson question is; **'What material is this?'** They will use a special piece of science equipment – a magnifier – to look very closely at materials, make observations and record what they see. Remind children, if necessary, how to use the magnifiers correctly.

Pupil workbook: Complete Activity 1: Describing glass, rock, brick and water on page 37.

The task

This is a two-part task, providing hands-on engagement with physical materials for part of the time and identification of materials around the classroom for the rest of the time. Groups should swap over half way through the time available.

Ask half the children to use magnifiers to examine the rock and brick samples in more detail. Show children how to use a magnifier in the correct way. Ask them what they can see. What do they notice about the materials when looking through a magnifier? Tell them to record their observations in sketch form.

Ask the other half of the children to label any other examples of the four materials, glass, brick, rock and water, found around the classroom. It is important that the children are supervised if there are other glass items that can be labelled. Ask children to make a list of other objects they can think of that are made from any of the four materials.

Pupil workbook: Complete Activity 2: Rock and brick on page 38 and Activity 3: Glass, water, rock or brick? on page 38.

Adaptations and support

Provide children requiring more focused support with one rock sample and one brick sample to observe closely and record. Encourage them to record only what they see through the magnifier by giving them a circular paper shape or paper with circles pre-printed on which to record.

Take it further

Children could identify and list other objects made of these four materials which are not found in the classroom. Provide a selection of pictures and catalogue pages with examples of objects made from the four materials to focus this task.

Reflect and review

Remind children of today's lesson question: **'What material is this?'**

Give children a selection of pictures with examples of the four materials from today's lesson cut out from Resource sheet: 1 Water or glass? and Resource sheet 2: Rocks or bricks? Include some pictures of metal, plastic and wood objects from Resource sheet 3: Wood, plastic or metal?. Tell them to sort the pictures into seven groups: water, glass, rock, brick, wood, metal and plastic.

Focus on the images of objects made from materials brick, rock, glass and water. Ask: How are the materials similar? How are they different? What properties do the materials have? Talk about how using a magnifier helped them observe the materials better. Encourage children to think about how the larger image reveals more detail.

Remind children of the terms mentioned in the 'Getting started' part of the lesson, 'natural' and 'manufactured', 'reuse' and 'recycle'. Ask: Which of the materials we learned about today is a natural material? Which have been changed into a manufactured material?

Ask: Which of these objects can be reused/used more than once? Are there any that can't be used more than once? For example, a paper bag or straw, a single-use plastic bag or beaker. What should we do with materials that can't be used again? Ensure that children understand, as a simple principle, that we should always try and recycle materials (if possible) and reduce their use, for example by not wasting paper, by using reusable straws, bags and beakers.

Remind them once more of the lesson question: **'What material is this?'** and consider responses from children that recognise the different properties, including whether materials can be reused or recycled.

Pupil workbook: Complete Activity 4: What material is this? on page 39.

Answers

Children should identify and group objects made of the same material, while recognising that materials of the same type can have very different properties, for example, rock and brick samples. They recognise that glass is usually smooth, shiny and see-through, but can be different colours, rock is mostly heavy, but can be rough or smooth, single-coloured or speckled.

Children should name rock and water as natural materials that are found in the environment in their natural state. They name glass and brick as manufactured because the natural materials they are made from have gone through a process to change them into a new material.

Homework suggestions

Suggest children go for a 'materials hunt' with a parent or carer. Find examples of how and where materials (learnt about in Lessons 1 and 2) are found and used in the local environment. For example, paving and walls made of rock, street lights and traffic lights made of metal and glass. Take photographs, make a list or draw some examples to share in school.

Assessment and evidence of learning

Children can:

- use a magnifier correctly
- identify glass, brick and rock in a range of objects
- sort objects made of these materials into groups and describe their properties
- recognise water in different places; in the natural world and the school and home contexts
- use appropriate vocabulary to describe observations and make comparisons of materials and objects
- explain that materials should be used carefully and can often be reused or recycled.

SNAP SCIENCE
GET YOUR TEETH INTO IT!
2nd EDITION

Lesson 3: Is all paper the same?

What children will learn and do

- Children learn that paper is a manufactured material made from wood, a natural source.
- They learn that there are different types of paper.
- They carry out a series of simple tests to identify the properties of different types of paper and their suitability for different uses.
- They sort types of paper into those that can be reused or recycled and those that can't.
- They answer the lesson question: **'Is all paper the same?'**

You will need

- collection of different types of paper: for example, writing paper (typical school quality), painting paper, wrapping paper, kitchen towel, greaseproof paper, wallpaper, sandpaper, magazine pages using glossy paper
- 'presents' wrapped in kitchen towel
- digital camera (or phone)
- sticky notes
- magnifiers, digital magnifier
- marker pens, wax crayons
- pipettes
- watercolour paints and brushes

Snap Science Year 1 Pupil Workbook

- pages 40–41

National Curriculum

Conceptual knowledge:

- identify and name a variety of everyday materials, [including wood, plastic, glass, metal, water and rock]

Working scientifically:

- performing simple tests

Scientific enquiry type:

- comparative testing

Key vocabulary	
Tier 2 vocabulary:	**Tier 3 vocabulary:**
compare, different, describe	observe, test
Adjectives to describe children's sensory explorations of materials' physical properties	absorb/absorbent, manufactured, material, natural, property, recycle, reuse

Health and safety Please refer to CLEAPSS for Health and Safety guidance and ensure that any identified hazards are managed appropriately.

Getting started

Remind children that during the last two lessons they learned about lots of different materials, made close observations and identified properties of those materials. Ask them to recall the names of the materials they learned about and give an example of an object that is made from that material.

Tell children they are going to investigate another material. Pass around samples of different types of paper. Tell them that paper is a manufactured material made from wood.

Ask: Do you like getting presents? Show children several 'presents' wrapped in kitchen towel. Show them a roll of kitchen towel and explain to them that the presents were very difficult to wrap using that paper. Pass the presents around the class and ask children to talk to the child sitting next to them about why they think their present was difficult to wrap. Take some responses and ask them what you should have done. Show them a selection of birthday and Christmas (if at the appropriate time of year) wrapping papers. Ask: Which paper would you rather receive a present wrapped in – kitchen towel or wrapping paper? Why might wrapping paper be better than kitchen towel?

Explain why it is important to recycle paper, so that it can be used again, in order to reduce the number of trees chopped down. Tell children there are some wrapping papers that are printed with plastic-based ink or have plastic in them and others that include foil (metal) and that those papers cannot be recycled. A useful test is the 'scrunch test'. If a sheet of paper crumples into a ball and stays in that form, then it is likely to be recyclable.

Tell children that today's lesson question is: **'Is all paper the same?'** They will use their scientific skills to test different papers and see whether they are suitable for different purposes.

The task

This task is made up of three tests that the children should try in turn. Explain that they are going to test different types of paper (such as kitchen paper, writing paper, greaseproof paper, glossy magazine paper and wrapping paper – printed or heavily decorated) and find out whether they can be used for painting on, writing on or for mopping up water. This task introduces the idea that the properties of a material make them suitable for a particular purpose.

Give children five paper samples to test. Tell them to:

1. Paint a face on each type of paper. Ask them to compare the paper samples and grade them according to which they think is the best for painting. Ask: How did you decide which was the best? And which was the worst? Why was that – what happened to the paper?
2. Write their name on each one using a pencil, a coloured marker and a wax crayon. Ask them to compare the papers and grade them according to which is the best to write on with each pen. Ask: How did you decide which was the best? And which was the worst? Which is the best combination of pen and paper? Which is the worst?
3. Drop water from a pipette onto each sample in turn. Ask them to compare the results and decide which paper sample they think is best to mop up some spilt water. Ask: How did you decide which was the best? And which was the worst? Did you count the drops? What other test could you do to find the paper that was best at mopping up?

Collect results after each test and collate on a simple table. Which paper did they decide was overall best for each task carried out. Ask: How do you know?

Pupil workbook: Complete Activity 1: The paper test on page 40.

Adaptations and support

Provide children requiring more focused support with fewer papers to test.

Take it further

Children could extend their testing of the papers' ability to mop up spills, and compare a paper towel (the likely best paper) with other materials that might be used for this purpose, for example a dishcloth and a tea towel.

Reflect and review

Remind children of today's lesson question: **'Is all paper the same?'**

Ask children what they learned from the tests they carried out. Were some types of paper better than others for particular tasks? Why? Remind children that they have used their working scientifically skills as they observed and compared what happened during the tests they carried out.

Encourage children to consider what they have learned about the different papers they have tested – especially those that they have agreed were the best for each purpose. For example, what particular properties of kitchen towel (likely best at mopping up) do they think made it the best for that job? They may refer to their observations of layers of paper, air pockets, thickness of the paper and so on. Introduce the idea that these particular features of kitchen towel make it especially useful for mopping up. If appropriate use the words absorb or absorbent as the paper towel's capacity for mopping up is discussed.

Remind children that paper is a material that we must use carefully, and that most types of paper can be recycled if it is not fit to be reused. Encourage them to sort the tested paper into two groups; paper to recycle and paper to reuse. Once this is done use the 'scrunch test' to check whether shiny or heavily decorated paper is likely to be suitable for recycling.

Remind them once more of the lesson question: **'Is all paper the same?'** and consider responses from children that recognise the many differences, including recyclability.

Pupil workbook: Complete Activity 2: What did you find out? on page 41.

Answers

Children should recognise and explain that there are many different types of papers with different properties.

Their tests show them that particular papers are useful for certain tasks because of their properties.

Children should understand in simple terms that paper should always be reused when possible and that most types of paper can be recycled, but that there are certain papers that cannot be recycled – those which include plastics or foil (metal).

Homework suggestions

Children could find out how many different types of paper there are at home? Talk to a parent or carer about the different types and how as a family they might use less paper, reuse or recycle whenever possible.

Assessment and evidence of learning

Children can:
- describe paper as a manufactured material made from wood, which is a natural source
- use correct names including 'kitchen towel', 'wrapping paper', 'writing paper', and so on, to name different types of paper
- explain how they tested the papers and compared their results
- suggest which type of paper was best for painting/writing on/mopping up, and give reasons
- refer to the results collected and suggest why properties of particular papers made them most useful for certain tasks.

Lesson 4: Is all fabric the same?

What children will learn and do

- Children learn that fabric is a manufactured material which can be made wholly or partly from different source materials, and therefore there are different types of fabric with different properties.
- They use magnifiers to look closely at different fabrics and make detailed drawings.
- They suggest why different fabrics are suitable for different types of clothing.
- They learn that fabrics can be made from recycled materials and should be reused or recycled whenever possible.
- They answer the lesson question: **'Is all fabric the same?'**

You will need

- commercially produced pack of fabrics or fabric samples, which includes natural fibres such as wool, cotton, bamboo (or similar), silk, fibre pile, poly cotton, breathable nylon, PVC coated nylon as well as fabric made from recycled sources
- selection of old clothing that can be cut into pieces, some of which are made from the fabrics listed above
- selection of clothing made from traditional fabrics or samples of fabric, particularly those that are culturally relevant to children
- collection of labels from clothing showing what the clothes are made from, including some of the fabrics listed above
- samples of fabric with a distinct weave or knit pattern (around six to choose from)
- magnifiers
- visualiser or digital microscope

If using the Snap Science Year 1 Pupil Workbook you may not require the resource sheet below.

Snap Science Year 1 Pupil Workbook

- pages 42–43

Snap Science Year 1 Digital subscription

- Resource sheet 1: What can you see?
- Snapshot 1: What is it made of?

Make sure you have opened/printed any *Snap* resources you intend to use in this lesson.

National Curriculum

Conceptual knowledge:

- identify and name a variety of everyday materials, [including wood, plastic, glass, metal water and rock]

Working scientifically:

- observing closely, using simple equipment.
- using observations and ideas to suggest answers to questions

Scientific enquiry type:

- identifying and classifying

Key vocabulary

Tier 2 vocabulary:	Tier 3 vocabulary:
compare, describe, different, similar, use	magnifier, observe, test
Adjectives to describe children's sensory explorations of materials' physical properties	material, natural, property, recycle, reuse

Health and safety Please refer to CLEAPSS for Health and Safety guidance and ensure that any identified hazards are managed appropriately.

Getting started

Remind children that in the last lesson they answered the lesson question: **'Is all paper the same?'** Prompt them to share what they learned then; that there are many different sorts of paper with different properties; and that tests they carried out showed them how the properties of those different papers made them useful for certain jobs, for example, kitchen paper has certain features that makes it useful for mopping up spills.

Tell children that in this lesson they are going to investigate another type of material, fabric, and answer the lesson question: **'Is all fabric the same?'** To do this they will be using their observation skills to look very closely at different fabrics, sometimes with only their eyes and sometimes through a magnifier. They will also use their sense of touch, to feel the differences between the samples they are handling.

Pass around a selection of fabric samples (including some traditional fabrics) and allow children to handle them. Ask them to tell the child next to them two things about their favourite fabric. Ask children for a selection of responses, modelling initially the type of response you are looking for, for example, 'I like this fabric. It is my favourite because it is bright and colourful, and feels smooth and strong'. Record words from the children's responses that describe the features of each fabric, such as soft, smooth, fluffy, and so on.

Explain to them that these samples are all different types of fabrics and write the names of the different types of fabric (such as wool, cotton, nylon, silk), together with the word 'fabric'. Ask children if they know which fabric might be which from those they have in front of them. Show them a sample of a distinctive type of fabric, such as wool. Describe its features; for example, 'Wool fabric is made from threads of sheep's wool. It is usually soft and can be fluffy.' Ask: Can we find a fabric that might be wool? If children struggle to find examples, point some out and then go on to look for examples of other types of fabric, including some that are made from plastic, for example, nylon or PVC. Show children an example of a fabric that has been made from recycled material (sports and other clothing is frequently made from recycled fabric waste). Tell them that fabric is not always made from natural materials, such as wool or cotton, but can also be made from recycled fabrics and other materials.

Explain to children that fabrics are made into many different things. Pass around some of the clothes samples. Ask them to describe the properties of the different fabrics and make simple comparisons of the clothing, for example, 'the fabric in this T-shirt is thinner than this sweatshirt'; 'this dress has silky fabric but this jumper is rough and scratchy.'

Revisit the lesson question once more: **'Is all fabric the same?'** and remind children that they will use their observation skills today as they carry out their task, look at fabrics in great detail and suggest what clothing they could be used for.

Pupil workbook: Complete Activity 1: Describing fabrics on page 42.

The task

Show children some of the clothing samples once again, for example, a T-shirt, a jumper, socks, trousers and a dress. Tell them to look at the clothes more closely and name the fabrics they are made from.

Give children a selection of samples of fabric with a distinct weave or knit pattern (around six to choose from). Ask them to look at three samples with a magnifier and draw what they see on Resource sheet 1:

What can you see? and cut out and stick a small piece of fabric next to each drawing. Ask them to suggest an item of clothing it might be used for.

Pupil workbook: Complete Activity 2: What can you see? on page 43.

Adaptations and support

Give the children three specific samples of fabric with a very obvious weave or knit pattern to observe.

Take it further

Encourage children to use what they have learned and suggest which fabric (from the fabric sample collection) might be best, for example, for clothing to wear on a hot day, if it might rain, or to keep us warm in winter.

Reflect and review

Ask children to compare their drawings of the fabric samples. Do they agree with the clothing uses suggested? Ask them to explain some of the choices made and prompt selected children (those that did the *Take it further* task) to share fabrics and clothing that might be suited to different weather conditions.

Explain to children that the tiny pieces of fabric they will have seen when looking at the fabrics with a magnifier are called fibres. Tell them that all the fabric samples are made of fibres that are put together (woven or knitted) in different patterns. Use a visualiser or similar to magnify images of items of clothing or fabric which show the weave in much greater detail and the fibres in close up.

Remind children once again that we must use all materials in our world very carefully and tell them that we can often reuse and recycle fabric used to make clothing in different ways; by using the clothing again, making it into something different or by making it into new fabrics. Suggest that families sometimes do this in schools by reusing school uniforms, either within a family or by passing clothing on at school (refer to any process in your setting that the children should be aware of).

Remind them once more of the lesson question: **'Is all fabric the same?'** and consider responses from children that recognise the many differences in properties across fabric types that determine how those fabrics might be used to make clothing.

Pupil workbook: Complete Activity 3: Reusing and recycling fabric on page 43.

Answers

Children should recognise and explain that there are many types of fabric with different names, for example, wool, cotton, nylon, PVC, and that these fabrics have different characteristics.

Their observations show them how fabrics vary and they recognise that different types of fabric with particular characteristics are used to make a variety of clothing.

Children understand in simple terms that much of the fabric used to make clothing can either be reused or recycled. They recognise why it is important to reuse clothing whenever possible by passing it on for use by others, giving the school-based process as an example of this.

Homework suggestions

Ask children: How many different types of fabric can you find at home? They could talk to a parent or carer about the fabrics used in their family's clothing and think about how any unwanted clothing might be reused or recycled.

Assessment and evidence of learning

Children can:

- use the word 'fabric' correctly in their discussions
- name a variety of source materials used to make fabrics, for example, plastic, nylon/polyester, cotton, wool
- use a magnifier correctly
- show details in their drawings
- use appropriate adjectives describe the properties of the fabric samples
- suggest appropriate clothing uses for each fabric.

If you are unsure after these four lessons that a child can identify and name a variety of everyday materials, including wood, plastic, glass, metal, water and rock you can use Snapshot activity 1: What is it made of?

Lesson 5: How can we group objects made of different materials?

What children will learn and do

- Children learn that objects can be made from more than one material.
- They sort objects into groups according to the material they are made from, and whether they are natural or manufactured materials.
- They answer the lesson question: **'How can we group objects made of different materials?'**

You will need

- collections of objects made from one, two or three of the basic list of materials from Lessons 1–4, that is, wood, metal, plastic, glass, rock, brick, water, paper and fabric. Objects made of a combination of materials might include toy cars, classroom scissors, paintbrushes, lamps (from electricity kit), spiral bound notepads
- labelled sorting hoops – sufficient for pairs of children to have at least four hoops
- sticky notes
- camera (optional)

If using the Snap Science Year 1 Pupil Workbook you may not require all of the resource sheets below.

Snap Science Year 1 Pupil Workbook

- pages 44–46

Snap Science Year 1 Digital subscription

- Resource sheet 1: What are they made from?
- Resource sheet 2: What materials are they?

Make sure you have opened/printed any *Snap* resources you intend to use in this lesson.

National Curriculum

Conceptual knowledge:

- distinguish between an object and the material from which it is made

Working scientifically:

- identifying and classifying

Scientific enquiry type:

- identifying and classifying

Key vocabulary	
Tier 2 vocabulary:	**Tier 3 vocabulary:**
compare, describe, different, similar, sort, use	group, observe
Adjectives to describe children's sensory explorations of materials' physical properties	manufactured, material, natural, properties

Health and safety Please refer to CLEAPSS for Health and Safety guidance and ensure that any identified hazards are managed appropriately.

Getting started

Remind children that over the last four lessons they have learned about many different types of material. Show children some of the objects from Lessons 1–4 (made of single materials only) and ask them to name the materials from which those objects are made: wood, metal, plastic, glass, rock, brick, water, paper and fabric.

Ask children: Can you remember which of these materials are natural materials? Which of them are manufactured materials? Ensure that they have a simple understanding of both terms and can place all materials into the correct categories.

Ask them to reorganise the objects into sorting hoops labelled with the material name. Discuss some of the groupings made. Ask: How are the plastic objects similar? How are they different? Model the type of response you are looking for, identifying some of the properties of the materials, 'The plastic objects are similar because they are mostly shiny and smooth. They are different because some are soft and bendy, and some are stiff and hard.'

Tell children that today they will be using their science skills to observe carefully, compare, sort and group objects in different ways.

Show them a toy that is made from a combination of two materials. Ask: What are the names of the materials from which this object is made? Where should this toy be put in the sorting hoops? Children should recognise that this presents a problem. How can they group objects made of more than one material using sorting hoops? Show them how to overlap the sorting hoops so that the toy can be in both the plastic and metal sorting hoops. Add to that example an object made from two materials which are different from the first object. Ask: Which materials is the object made from? Where should it be placed in the sorting hoops?

Tell children that today's lesson question is: **'How can we group objects made of different materials?'** Remind them that they will use their science skills as they observe carefully, compare, sort and group objects in different ways.

Pupil workbook: Complete Activity 1: Natural or manufactured? on page 44.

The task

Explain to children that they are going to sort a collection of objects made from more than one material and identify the materials that each object is made of. In pairs, children should sort ten objects made from two or three materials, drawn from a larger group collection of around fifteen objects.

Show children Resource sheet 1: What are they made from? Model how to complete the table, starting with the two suggested objects, a serving spoon (made of plastic and wood) and classroom scissors (made of metal and plastic), ticking the materials from which each object is made, then listing the other objects in the first column (with help as needed) and ticking materials for those objects too.

Provide each pair with four sorting hoops and sticky notes to use as labels. Ask them if they can place the objects they have listed in two or three overlapping sorting hoops.

Pupil workbook: Complete Activity 2: Objects made from more than one material on page 45 and Activity 3: Sorting objects on page 46.

Adaptations and support

Give children four objects made from two materials. Ask them to identify the two materials and, using the names from Resource sheet 2: What materials are they? and with adult help as appropriate, label each object with the names of the materials from which it is made. Ask them if they can put any of the objects into overlapping sorting hoops. Take photographs of the labelling and sorting.

Take it further

Encourage children to build on their list of ten objects, identifying and adding to their list objects from the classroom and beyond that contain more than three materials, for example, a climbing frame, bicycle or even a car. Ask them to sketch their chosen object and label it with some of the materials that they think it is made from. Children can use information books to carry out research and discover more about the materials used to make these objects.

Reflect and review

Ask pairs of children to show how they sorted their objects into hoops. It may be necessary to help them with this, especially where children are trying to overlap three rather than two material hoops.

Once again, check that children can correctly name the different materials the objects are made from. Find out whether there were any objects that they struggled to place. Was that because they weren't sure what materials the objects were made from or for another reason?

Ask children why they think that objects are sometimes made of two or more materials. For example, why has a spoon got a wooden handle and a metal bowl part? Encourage the children to link the particular properties of the materials making up the object to potential uses. The link between material properties and their suitability (fit for purpose) will be explored more fully in Module 4.

Remind children once more of the lesson question: **'How can we group objects made of different materials?'**

Answers

Children recognise and can name the materials learned about in previous lessons which are used to make objects, grouping them together in sorting rings. Where more than one material is present in an object they know how to overlap sorting rings to indicate that objects in the overlap are made of two (or three) materials.

Children name and group wood, rock and water as natural materials that are found in the environment in their natural state. They name and group metal, plastic, glass, brick, paper and fabric as manufactured.

Homework suggestions

Ask children to find at home an object made of three or more materials? Then take a photograph or draw it and add labels to show the different materials.

Assessment and evidence of learning

Children can:
- recognise and name different types of materials
- complete the table correctly
- suggest reasons why an object might have been made from more than one type of material
- suggest how and why a particular material is used in an object
- sort objects according to their source material, recognising when overlapping sorting rings are needed for objects made of several materials
- sort objects made of single materials as natural and manufactured, explaining in simple terms why they belong to each group.

Children will have further opportunities in Module 4 to consolidate their understanding and demonstrate that they have met the conceptual knowledge statement for this lesson so there should be no need to use a Snapshot at this point in the module.

Module 4: Properties and uses of materials

Lesson 1: Can the same object be made from different materials?

What children will learn and do

- Children learn that objects are made from one or more different materials.
- They sort objects made from metal, wood and plastic in different ways, including by type of material or use.
- They learn to record their observations in a table, writing their own column headings.
- They learn that materials should be used carefully and can often be reused or recycled.
- They answer the lesson question: **'Can the same object be made from different materials?'**

You will need

- metal, wooden and reusable plastic spoons
- paperclips made of different materials
- beakers made of different materials – no single-use plastics
- toys made of different single materials, for example all wood
- shoes and sandals made of, for example, plastic, fabric, leather, rubber
- selection of objects made of two or more materials
- samples of toy bricks and bricks used in buildings
- china, plastic and single-use paper plates
- sorting hoops and labels

If using the Snap Science Year 1 Pupil Workbook you may not require all of the resource sheets below.

Snap Science Year 1 Pupil Workbook

- pages 47–48

Snap Science Year 1 Digital subscription

- Resource sheet 1: What different materials are they made from?
- Resource sheet 2: What different materials are they made from?
- Snapshot activity 1: What is it made of?

Make sure you have opened/printed any *Snap* resources you intend to use in this lesson.

National Curriculum

Conceptual knowledge:

- distinguish between an object and the material from which it is made

Working scientifically:

- observing closely, [using simple equipment]
- gathering and recording data to help in answering questions

Scientific enquiry type:

- identifying and classifying

Key vocabulary	
Tier 2 vocabulary:	**Tier 3 vocabulary:**
compare, different, similar, sort, suitable, use	group, observe
Adjectives and comparatives to describe properties of materials.	material, property, recycle, reuse

Health and safety Please refer to CLEAPSS for Health and Safety guidance and ensure that any identified hazards are managed appropriately.

Getting started

Remind children about the lessons in Module 3 Naming and describing materials, where they explored some natural and manufactured materials and learned about the importance of reducing, reusing and recycling materials. Can they remember which materials they learned about? (Wood, plastic, metal, water, glass, paper, fabric.)

Lay out three sorting hoops labelled 'metal', 'wood' and 'plastic'. Place a selection of objects (made from one material only) in a large carry box. Show children what is in the box.

Select one object made from metal, wood or plastic and ask in which hoop it should be placed. Next, select a glass beaker. Ask: Where do you think this glass beaker should be placed, without adding another hoop? Place it outside the three hoops.

Pick out more objects that fit into one of the three hoops, emphasising each time why the object fits into its hoop, explaining that you are organising them into different types of materials. Then select a notebook with a card cover and ask where it should be placed. Place it with the glass beaker outside the three hoops.

Continue choosing objects that fit into the three hoops with help from the children. Then select a china plate. Explain that this sorting is not very tidy, with several objects now outside the hoops. Ask: Can you think of another way to sort these three objects? Encourage them to identify a property that is similar to each of the objects currently outside the hoops (as they are all made from different materials) such as, 'They are all hard', or 'They are all smooth'. Add a hoop and label it with that property.

Place a wooden toy, a plastic toy and a fabric toy together in a new hoop. Ask: What is similar about all of these objects? What do they have in common? Help children to recognise that the three objects are all toys, and their use is 'for playing'. Add a new label for this hoop.

Tell the children that today's lesson question is: **'Can the same object be made from different materials?'** Explain that they will be using their science skills to observe, compare, sort and group objects by their names and what they are used for, such as a beaker for drinking and a toy for playing, and that they will also identify the materials from which each object is made.

The task

Give small groups of children a selection of four types of objects, e.g. beakers, spoons, shoes and toys, made from different single materials. Give them Resource sheet 2: What different materials are they made from? Ask the children to group their objects according to their name (i.e. beaker, toy) and what they are used for, and to identify the material from which each object is made, adding that information to their table of results as they go.

Tell children to look at their tables of results with a partner. Focus on one type of object, such as beakers. Ask: What do you notice about the materials the beakers are made from? What different materials were there? How do these materials compare? Do you think that the materials were chosen to make the object useful in some way?

Ask children to describe the properties of the materials used for the objects and tell their partner why they are a good material to make the object from.

Pupil workbook: Complete Activity 1: What materials are they made from? on page 47.

Adaptations and support

Give children a reduced number of objects made from a single material that fit into the groupings of spoons, paperclips and plates. Give them Resource sheet 1: What different materials are they made from? Ask the children to group their objects by name and what they are used for, and then fill in the table by ticking the materials from which they are made.

Take it further

Include objects made from more than one material in some selections of objects, for example, a spoon made from wood and metal, a shoe with a rubber sole and fabric upper. Ask children to think about why different materials have been used for different parts of the object. Tell them to draw one of the objects, and add labels to explain the suitability of different materials being used for different parts.

Reflect and review

Show children a plastic plate and a china plate. Ask children to talk to their partners about the plates and why they think the plastic plate might be better for young children to use. Ask: Can you think of a material that would not be good to make a plate? Why do you think that?

Show children examples of single-use paper and plastic (single-use if still available and reusable) plates. Ask: When would these be used? Why would they be useful? Remind children about reusing and recycling materials whenever possible. Tell them it is important to use single-use plastic (in particular) as little as possible. This is an example where single-use plastic plates should not be used. Paper plates are a better alternative as they can often be recycled or are biodegradable. Better still on a picnic, for example, to take washable plastic plates that can be used over and over again.

Show children a real brick and some plastic and wooden bricks. Ask children to talk to their partners about which is most suitable (best) for them to use in the classroom for building and which is better for building outside. Ask: What properties make a brick suitable for its use?

Show children several objects made from more than one material from the selections investigated by those who carried out the *Take it further* task. Ask several of those children to share their ideas about why different materials have been used for different parts of these objects. Ensure that the idea that the materials' properties make them more useful for one part of the object rather than the whole object comes through in the discussion.

Remind children once more of the lesson question: **'Can the same objects be made from different materials?'**

Pupil workbook: Complete Activity 2: Which should I use? on page 48.

Answers

Children recognise and can name types of objects that can be made from a variety of different materials and can describe the features of the materials used. For example, spoons can be made of plastic, metal and wood. The spoons share some features – they are all hard and rigid – but the metal spoon feels cool to the touch and heavy compared to the wood and plastic spoons, which feel warmer and lighter.

They can explain in simple terms how the properties of a material makes an object more useful for a particular purpose and give some examples, such as a reusable plastic beaker is better to take on a picnic in case it is dropped. A glass or china beaker might break and feels heavier to carry.

Homework suggestions

Ask children to carry out a 'Hat hunt' at home. Talk with a parent or carer about what they find and talk about why different materials are used in a winter hat, a cycle helmet, a sun hat, hood on a rain coat, etc. A range of hats will be used in the next lesson so ask children to bring one in from home.

Assessment and evidence of learning

Children can:
- correctly name wooden, glass and plastic objects and put them in the right groups
- identify when an object is made from more than one material
- re-sort objects using a different criterion other than the material from which it is made.

When comparing objects made from different materials, children can:
- write the correct heading on the table
- complete the table correctly
- suggest why different materials might be used to make the same object
- suggest why some materials are not suitable for making a particular object.

If you are unsure if a child can distinguish between an object and the material it is made from you can use the Snapshot activity 1: What is it made of?

Lesson 2: What properties do materials have?

What children will learn and do

- Children learn that materials have physical properties that make them useful for different purposes.
- They use a feely bag to distinguish between properties that can be identified by touch and by sight.
- They answer the lesson question: **'What properties do materials have?'**

You will need

- three toys, three beakers and three hats – either ones that children have brought in from home (last lesson's homework activity) or ones you have provided
- selection of samples of materials including wood, metal, plastic (not single-use), glass, rock, brick, water, paper and fabric
- sorting hoops
- property words from Resource sheet 1 Words for properties of materials, enlarged on card to use as sorting hoop labels
- camera
- feely bags

If using the Snap Science Year 1 Pupil Workbook you may not require all of the resource sheets below.

Snap Science Year 1 Pupil Workbook

- pages 49–50

Snap Science Year 1 Digital subscription

- Resource sheet 1: Words for properties of materials
- Resource sheet 2: What properties does a material have?
- Snapshot activity 1: What are my properties?

Make sure you have opened/printed any *Snap* resources you intend to use in this lesson.

National Curriculum

Conceptual knowledge:

- describe the simple physical properties of a variety of everyday materials

Working scientifically:

- observing closely, [using simple equipment]
- using their observations and ideas to suggest answers to questions

Scientific enquiry type:

- identifying and classifying

Key vocabulary	
Tier 2 vocabulary:	**Tier 3 vocabulary:**
different, sort, record, use	group, observe
Adjectives and comparatives to describe properties of materials.	opaque, property, transparent

Health and safety Please refer to CLEAPSS for Health and Safety guidance and ensure that any identified hazards are managed appropriately.

Getting started

Remind children that last science lesson they used their science skills to observe, sort and group objects made of different materials. Place a selection of objects made of single materials, for example, three toys, three beakers and three hats in a 'muddle' in a position where children can see them. Ask: How many different ways can you sort and group these objects? Children should recall that the objects were sorted in three ways in the last lesson: by name – toys, beakers, hats; by material, such as plastic, glass, fabric, wool; by use – for playing with, for holding liquid, for covering the head.

Tell children that today they will be using their science skills and their senses as they observe and group materials in yet another way and will answer the lesson question: **'What properties do materials have?'**

Give out a variety of material samples: wood, metal, plastic, glass, rock, brick, water, paper and fabric. Have enough materials for at least one sample between two children. Ask them to talk to the child next to them about how their material feels and looks. Encourage children to use the words that are listed on Resource sheet 1: Words for physical properties of materials. Collect answers from the children and display relevant words writing them under the headings 'Feels' and 'Looks'.

Explore children's understanding of the words listed on Resource sheet 1 more fully. Tell them to stand up if they think they have a smooth material. Ask them to name the material and identify other materials that share the same property. Model the type of response you are looking for, for example 'this block of wood is smooth. So are the plastic, and the metal materials'. Repeat this using other words from those listed.

Ask children if they have a material with two of these physical properties, for example, a material that is both shiny and hard.

Finally, show children a piece of wood. Ask: What are the properties of this piece of wood? Encourage children to come up with as many property words as possible, using their senses to explore and describe how the material feels and looks. Remind children once more of the lesson question **'What properties do materials have?'**

Pupil workbook: Complete Activity 1: How does the material look and feel? on page 49.

The task

Explain to children that their task involves playing a game using materials from previous lessons. They have to describe a hidden material to a partner using 'property' words only. The partner has to work out what that material might be.

Children work in pairs or threes. Give each pair a feely bag and a box of material samples. Children take it in turns to select (out of view) a material sample from the box and place it in the feely bag. They use property words to describe the material as they touch it inside the bag, for example 'this material is smooth on one side but rough on the other'. The other child (or children if working in threes) must suggest what the material could be based on the property words used. Tell children, with support as appropriate, to record the names of the materials in the right boxes on Resource sheet 2: What properties does a material have? according to the properties they have identified. Ask: Which materials have more than one property? Which properties often go together?

Pupil workbook: Complete Activity 2: What material is it? on page 50.

Adaptations and support

Provide children with a selection of materials that have most or all of the properties on Resource sheet 1: Words for properties of materials, three sorting hoops and property labels. Encourage them to use a hoop at a time, select a label, choose materials that share a property and describe the groups they have made, for example 'the materials in this hoop are all soft – that is a property they share'. Take photographs of their groupings to check understanding.

Take it further

Encourage children to think about the properties of the materials they have explored and suggest how these properties make the material more or less useful for a particular purpose. Tell them to think about three of the materials, wood, metal, plastic, glass, rock, brick, water, paper or fabric. Ask them to draw and write their ideas, prompting their thinking by asking; What job might (for example) wood be used for? What properties make it useful? Could glass or paper be used for the same thing?

Reflect and review

Tell children to look at each other's sorting records. Do they agree with each other's sorting? Ask: Which properties can you identify by feeling and which by looking? Which properties often seem to go together?

Revisit some examples of materials to check that property words are understood by all children. Once again, as necessary, model the use of property words in a simple descriptive sentence about the materials. Ask children if they know the special science words for materials that are see-through and that cannot be seen through. Add the words to the list on display (if not already there). Substitute labelled name cards 'transparent' and 'opaque' for the 'see-through' and 'can't see through' cards, respectively.

Remind children that they have been using their science skills to investigate the properties of different materials. Ask children who completed the *Take it further* task, to talk about some of the materials they looked at and suggest what purpose the materials could be used for (or not).

Remind children of the lesson question, **'What properties do materials have?'** and consider responses from children that demonstrate knowledge of the names of materials, their properties (and associated vocabulary) and, in simple terms, how physical properties can make a material useful.

Answers

Children use the word 'property' to describe how a material looks and feels. For example, they might say 'this block of wood is smooth, hard and warm to the touch. These are some of its properties'.

They use specific vocabulary to describe properties correctly and can give examples of properties shared by different materials. For example, they might say 'this block of wood is smooth and hard, so are the plastic and the metal blocks'.

Homework suggestions

Children could look for some transparent materials at home. What objects are made from them?

Assessment and evidence of learning

Children can:
- use appropriate property-related vocabulary and the term 'property' correctly
- recognise that materials can have more than one property
- complete the table correctly.

If you are unsure if a child can describe the simple physical properties of a variety of everyday materials you can use Snapshot activity 1: What are my properties?

Lesson 3: Does it bend or stretch?

What children will learn and do

- Children learn that some materials bend or stretch, while others do not, and that this makes them useful for different purposes.
- They carry out a stretch test on a variety of materials.
- They learn how to collect and present results of their test in a paper strip bar chart.
- They answer the lesson question: **'Does it bend or stretch?'**

You will need

- selection of objects from previous lessons that are rigid and do not bend, stretch, squash or twist
- sufficient single socks for each child (in groups of three) to have a different sock to test
- modelling clay, pipe cleaners, 3D shapes
- stretchy clothing, such as, tights, lycra leggings, leotards and sports tops
- rubber bands
- paper strips, scissors, large sheets of paper to stick the strips on

Snap Science Year 1 Pupil Workbook

- pages 51–52

National Curriculum

Conceptual knowledge:

- compare and group together a variety of everyday materials on the basis of their simple properties

Working scientifically:

- performing simple tests
- using their observations and ideas to suggest answers to questions
- gathering and recording data to help in answering questions

Scientific enquiry type:

- comparative testing

Key vocabulary	
Tier 2 vocabulary:	**Tier 3 vocabulary:**
compare, record, use	bar chart, observe
Adjectives and comparatives to describe properties of materials.	bend, flexible, property, rigid

Health and safety Please refer to CLEAPSS for Health and Safety guidance and ensure that any identified hazards are managed appropriately.

Getting started

Begin by drawing children's attention to the property words that were listed (displayed) during the last lesson. Ask children if they remember the word that is used to describe how something 'looks' and 'feels'. These are known as the properties of a material. Add this word to the display (if it is not already there).

Give every child an object that is rigid (select from those used in previous lessons). For example, objects made of wood, metal, plastic, glass, rock and brick, including toys, shoes, hats, beakers, spoons and classroom equipment. Ask children to talk to their partner about the material from which the object is made and describe some of its properties.

Ask children to put their objects on the floor in front of them and stand up. Tell them to pick up the object. Watch how children bend down as they do this. Some will bend their backs, some will bend their knees, and some might even kneel down. Select some children who bent their backs. Tell them to stand up and pick up the object in the same way as before. Ask the rest of the children what these children did to pick up their object. Repeat with some children who bent their knees. Ask them how they can describe what they had to do to their backs and their knees to be able to pick up the object. Add words they use to the display prompting them, where necessary, with the words 'bend', 'bending' and 'bent'. Ask children to sit with their arms folded and legs crossed. Ask: What parts of your bodies are bent now? Tell children that the scientific word to describe something that can bend and not break is flexible. Things that do not bend are rigid. Add these property words to the display. Ask: Can any of the objects you have in front of you bend? Can you think of anything else in the classroom that is flexible? Which materials are flexible objects made from?

Next, ask children to stand up and reach up in the air as far as they can with their fingers. Ask them to sit down. What words can they think of to describe what they did when they reached up? Add words they use to the display. It may be necessary to prompt them to say 'stretch' by stretching a rubber band. Hold the rubber band in both hands, stretch it and then bring the hands together. Do not let go from one hand. Draw children's attention to what happens to the rubber band as it is stretched and released. They should notice that it goes back to the same length and shape as before it was stretched. Add the word stretchy to the property words display. Ask: Can you think of anything in the classroom that stretches? Which materials are stretchy objects made from?

Tell children that today they will be using their science skills to carry out a comparative test, make observations and record their results in a bar chart. Explain to children that they are going to see what happens when objects are stretched and bent in different ways. They will answer the lesson question **'Does it bend or stretch?'**

The task

Organise the children to work in threes. Give them a different type of sock each and two paper strips. Explain to them that they are going to test how far each sock can stretch. They may need adult help during parts of this task.

Tell them to cut a paper strip the same length as their sock before stretching. Ask one child to hold the sock being tested in both hands and stretch it as far as they can. Another child holds up a new paper strip beside the stretched sock and the third child cuts it equivalent to the length of the stretched sock. Label the strips (Before stretching or After stretching Sock 1, 2 or 3). After they have carried out their tests show them how to stick the paper strips next to one another to form a bar chart of results. Ask: What happened to each sock? What happened when you stopped stretching the sock? Did it go back to its starting size? Which sock stretched the most? Which stretched the least?

Pupil workbook: Complete Activity 1: Stretch test on page 51 and Activity 2: Test results on page 52.

Adaptations and support

Give selected children pipe cleaners, modelling clay, cylinders, cuboids and triangular prism shapes. Ask them to roll some of the modelling clay into long strips. Tell them to wrap the modelling clay and pipe cleaners around the 3D shapes, as this will make it easier to form shapes. Ask: What are these materials called? What have you been able to do to the materials you have been using? How are they different? The modelling clay can be stretched and bent, but only so far, as it will break if stretched too much. The pipe cleaners can only be bent. What property words can you use to describe what you observed?

Take it further

Provide children with a variety of stretchy clothing (as well as socks) to test, such as tights, lycra leggings, leotards and tops. Ask them to work in pairs and carry out a simple stretch test, taking measurements before and after using paper strips or a ruler (if appropriate). Ask: Which of the things you tested stretched the most? How do you know? What did you notice happening to the material as it was stretched? What property words can you use to describe the materials that the clothing is made from?

Reflect and review

Ask children to share their stretch test paper strip bar graphs with the class – these could be tacked to the wall or photographed, then shared on screen. Encourage several children to talk about the results they recorded (include those that looked at a wider range of clothing as well as at socks). Ask: What does this bar chart show? Which object that you tested stretched the most? What did you observe happening to the object when it was stretched? What happened to the object when it was not being stretched any more? How does being stretchy – one of the properties of these materials – make them useful for the job they do? Look for answers from children that mention a variety of uses, such as, stretching to fit around a body part; fitting people with different size feet; making moving while wearing the clothing easier, using as a sports kit.

Remind children that all the materials that they tested stretched (some more and some less than others). Other materials do not stretch when pulled, but can bend. Ask children who worked with clay and pipe cleaners to compare those two materials. Ask them to describe what they learned, ensuring they make the point that pipe cleaners are flexible; they form and keep their shape when the 3D shape is removed. They can be straightened out and made flat, but they will still be the same length as before. They are not stretchy.

Tell children to look at the object given to them at the beginning of the lesson. Do any of those objects or materials bend or stretch without breaking? Tell children that the word to describe a material that does not bend or stretch is rigid.

Remind children of the lesson question, 'Does it bend or stretch?' and consider responses from children that demonstrate knowledge of these and other properties (and associated vocabulary) and, in simple terms, that these and other physical properties can make a material useful.

Pupil workbook: Complete Activity 3: Flexible or rigid? on page 52.

Answers

Children can use vocabulary appropriately to describe physical properties. For example, they might say 'this fabric stretches when it's pulled, but this wooden bowl cannot be stretched or bent. This pipe cleaner bends to wrap around a shape, but it doesn't stretch'.

They recognise and can suggest in simple terms what makes stretchy materials useful for certain purposes, e.g. in making clothing, including sportswear. For example, they might say 'my woolly hat is stretchy so that I can pull it over my head. It's thick and woolly, so it keeps my head warm'.

Homework suggestions

Children could test their socks at home. Which are the stretchiest?

Assessment and evidence of learning

When describing the properties and uses of materials, children:

- use appropriate property-related vocabulary to describe the physical properties of materials
- suggest how the properties of materials might make them useful for certain purposes.

When carry out the stretch test or investigating pipe cleaners, children can:
- follow instructions to carry out the test
- construct a paper strip bar chart showing the results of their test correctly
- use the results to make comparisons of materials tested, for example, identifying which material stretched the most and the least.

SNAP SCIENCE
GET YOUR TEETH INTO IT!
2nd EDITION

Lesson 4: Do all materials get wet?

What children will learn and do

- Children learn that some materials are absorbent, while others are not, and that this makes them useful for different purposes.
- They test a variety of materials to identify them as absorbent, not absorbent or waterproof.
- They record their observations in a table.
- They answer the lesson question: **'Do all materials get wet?'**

You will need

- example of waterproof clothing
- selection of waterproof and non-waterproof fabrics including PVC-coated nylon or other waterproof fabrics – cut into squares big enough to sit on top of small beakers
- absorbent and non-absorbent papers – cut into squares
- water droppers
- 2p coin-sized plastic counters
- small transparent beakers
- water
- food colouring

If using the Snap Science Year 1 Pupil Workbook you may not require the resource sheet below.

Snap Science Year 1 Pupil Workbook

- pages 53–54

Snap Science Year 1 Digital subscription

- Resource sheet 1: Do all materials get wet?
- Snapshot activity 1: What are my properties?
- Snapshot activity 2: Comparing and grouping materials

Make sure you have opened/printed any *Snap* resources you intend to use in this lesson.

National Curriculum

Conceptual knowledge:

- compare and group together a variety of everyday materials on the basis of their simple properties

Working scientifically:

- performing simple tests
- gathering and recording data to help in answering questions

Scientific enquiry type:

- comparative testing

Key vocabulary	
Tier 2 vocabulary:	**Tier 3 vocabulary:**
compare, record, use	observe, test
Adjectives and comparatives to describe properties of materials.	absorb/absorbent, property, waterproof

Health and safety Please refer to CLEAPSS for Health and Safety guidance and ensure that any identified hazards are managed appropriately.

Getting started

Remind children of the last few lessons' focus on the properties of materials. Ask: Can anyone remember what the word 'property' means? Encourage children to suggest properties of different materials that make them useful, recalling examples and property words from previous lessons. If needed, model the type of response you are looking for, for example, 'The classroom window is made of transparent glass. It is smooth and rigid too'; 'This ruler is made of plastic. It is flexible, can bend, but does not stretch'. Add any property words not already added to the display.

To explore children's understanding of properties of materials still further, pose some 'What if...?' scenarios. Ask children whether they think your ideas are 'Silly or Sensible?' and to explain their thinking. For example, 'What if the classroom door was made of paper? Why might that be a silly idea, why might it be a sensible idea?', 'What if my hat for playground duty was made of metal?, Why might that be a silly idea, why might it be a sensible idea?', 'What if your socks were made of plastic?, Why might that be a silly idea, why might it be a sensible idea?' and so on. Encourage children to focus on the properties of the material in question and the purpose that the object is being used for. Is the material a suitable choice or not?

Tell children that in this lesson they will be using their science skills to test a property of some materials - whether they 'soak up' or 'keep out' water. You can introduce the science terms absorbent and waterproof to describe these properties and use them alongside or instead of everyday language.

Show children examples of different papers and fabrics, some in the form of items of clothing – at this point do not include examples of kitchen towel or other absorbent paper or fabric.

'Accidentally' knock over a plastic beaker containing a small amount of water. Try to use a piece of heavily-printed magazine paper (likely to be waterproof) and a piece of waterproof fabric to attempt to mop it up. Ask: Do you think this is working? Can you suggest something I could use instead?

Explain to children that they are going to observe, compare and test to find out how well different materials soak up/absorb water and which materials keep out water/are waterproof, as they investigate the lesson question: **'Do all materials get wet?'**

To carry out their test children will use water droppers. If children have not used a water dropper before, you might wish to include a practice task, so that they can learn how to fill the dropper and drop water carefully onto a surface. Provide 2p coin-sized counters or similar for them to use to practise, encouraging them to cover the surface slowly with drops.

The task

Give children, working in pairs, a mixed selection of fabrics and papers (eight to ten samples), cut into squares that are large enough to cover the top of a small (ideally clear) beaker. Ensure that there are samples within the material selection that 'do not let water through' (waterproof), 'soak up' water (absorbent), and 'let water through' (not waterproof). You might add a few drops of food colouring to the water the children use so that the movement of the water is easier to see.

Each pair should choose four materials from the selection to test, placing each sample in turn on top of the small beaker and using the water dropper to carefully drop water onto the sample's surface. They should complete Resource sheet 1: Do all materials get wet? to record their results, by sticking a fabric sample, drawing and/or writing their observations of each material tested in the appropriate column and box.

Ask: How will you know which materials let water through and which do not? Which materials stopped the water going through completely – are waterproof? Which materials soaked up the water drops – are absorbent? Which materials that you haven't tested do you think might be waterproof? What makes you think that? Which might be absorbent and useful for mopping up a spill? What makes you think that?

Pupil workbook: Complete Activity 1: Absorbency test on page 53.

Adaptations and support

Give children four carefully selected material samples to test, ensuring that at least one sample is waterproof and one is absorbent. Support them, as needed, to record the results of their test on Resource sheet 1: Do all materials get wet? Check understanding of terms used by asking: What happens to the water if a material is absorbent? Where does the water go? What happens if a material is waterproof? Where does the water go?

Take it further

Ask children to carry out a further test on materials that they have found to be absorbent – How wet can these materials get? Suggest that they should try to use their water droppers more carefully as they add drops of water to the absorbent materials. Tell them to measure how much water they are adding by counting drops, full or half-full droppers of water, and to write down their results as they go. Ask: How do you know that the water has been absorbed? What happens when the material can no longer absorb water? (It is fully saturated.) Which material absorbed the most water?

Reflect and review

Select several children to describe to others what they did and what they found out as they explored the lesson question **'Do all materials get wet?'** Prompt children to think about the tests they carried out as they look at the results they recorded on Resource sheet 1. Ask: Which materials did you test? Were any of your materials waterproof? How did you know that they were waterproof? Children should respond with a simple explanation, for example 'the water didn't go through, it stayed on top of the material'.

Check for understanding by asking them to suggest other materials that might be waterproof and explain what makes them think that. Ask: Did any of your materials absorb water? How do you know they were absorbent? Listen out for simple explanations such as, 'the water soaked into the material, we could see that the fabric was wet'. Ask: Did any of your materials let all the water through? If none did, then ask children to suggest what type of material might do that – likely to be a very thin or an open weave material.

Remind children that these (and other) properties of materials make them useful for particular purposes or tasks. Check their understanding once more by asking: What sort of clothes do you think waterproof fabrics would be good for? Where would it be useful to have paper or another material that absorbs water well?

Pupil workbook: Complete Activity 2: Waterproof or absorbent? on page 54.

Answers

Children use vocabulary appropriately to describe physical properties, using terms waterproof and absorbent where appropriate. For example, 'This fabric is absorbent. I know that because the water soaks into it'; 'This fabric is waterproof. I know that because the water does not soak in, it runs off or sits in drops on it'.

They recognise and can suggest in simple terms what makes waterproof and absorbent materials useful for certain purposes. For example, 'This waterproof material could be used for an umbrella, because the rain won't go through'; 'This fabric would be great for mopping up spills, because the liquid soaks into it'.

Homework suggestions

Children could look at home for absorbent and waterproof materials. What are they used for?

Assessment and evidence of learning

When describing the properties and uses of materials, children can:

- use appropriate property-related vocabulary to describe the physical properties of materials
- explain how they know that a material absorbs water or is waterproof
- suggest how absorbent and waterproof properties might make material useful for certain purposes.

When testing a variety of materials they can:

- make observations and comparisons of those materials, for example, identifying which materials absorb water and which don't
- correctly record their results in a table.

If you are unsure if a child can compare materials, identifying differences and similarities in physical properties and linking these to possible uses, you can use the Snapshot activity 1: What are my properties? and/or Snapshot activity 2: Comparing and grouping materials.

Module 5: Animals (vertebrates)

Lesson 1: Who's who in the animal world?

What children will learn and do

- Children learn that there are five vertebrate groups in the animal kingdom: mammals, amphibians, reptiles, birds and fish.
- They group animals using their own sorting criteria.
- They learn that reptiles are one of the vertebrate groups and that the things that make them distinct are: eggs, claws, teeth, scaly skin and living on land.
- They answer the lesson question: **'Who's who in the animal world?'**

You will need

Snap Science Year 1 Pupil Workbook

- pages 55–56

Snap Science Year 1 Digital subscription

- Slideshow 1: Who's who
- Slideshow 2: Reptiles

Make sure you have opened/printed any *Snap* resources you intend to use in this lesson.

Prepare sets of 26 animal cards using slides 8–14 from Slideshow 1 (the numbered pictures including the names), with one set of cards for each group of between four and six children. These cards will be used in every lesson in the module and need to be stored between lessons.

All children will need access to the reptile 'posters' in Slideshow 2. It is not essential to print these, but children will need to be able to study the images closely.

National Curriculum

Conceptual knowledge:

- identify and name a variety of common animals including [fish, amphibians,] reptiles, [birds and mammals]
- identify and name a variety of common animals that are carnivores, herbivores and omnivores
- describe and compare the structure of a variety of common animals ([fish, amphibians,] reptiles, [birds and mammals,] including pets)

Working scientifically:

- observing closely, [using simple equipment]

Scientific enquiry type:

- identifying and classifying

Key vocabulary	
Tier 2 vocabulary:	**Tier 3 vocabulary:**
features, structure	group, identify
	amphibian, bird, diet, fish, mammal, reptile, vertebrate

Health and safety Please refer to CLEAPSS for Health and Safety guidance and ensure that any identified hazards are managed appropriately.

Getting started

Talk with children about animals they know. Which ones have they seen? Where have they seen them? In real life or on a screen? Do they have any animals at home? Collect their suggestions in a list as they will be referred to within the rest of the lesson and subsequent lessons.

If all the suggested animals are mammals, ask children if they know of any animals that don't have fur.

Tell children that animals are split into different groups depending on their features and their structure, and that today they are going to answer the question: **'Who's who in the animal world?'** Tell them that the focus of this module will be on a big group of animals called vertebrates. Tell them that all these animals all have a backbone.

Present Slideshow 1: Who's who. Show slides 1–7 and ask children to name the animals shown. Note any animals that were in the list generated by children earlier.

Then present slides 8–14, which show the same photographs but labelled with the animals' names. Focus on names of animals that were not known by the class.

Put children in groups of four to six. Provide a set of cards for each group, created using print-outs of slides 8–14 of Slideshow 1: Who's who. Ask children to group the animal cards as they wish and then tell the class their reasons for grouping them that way.

Explain that every scientist working with animals groups them in the same ways according to their structure and features they have in common. Tell children that some of these groups are: birds, amphibians, reptiles, fish and mammals.

Present slides 15–20 of Slideshow 1: Who's who, and ask children to compare their groupings with the ones on the slides.

Ask children to discuss briefly, in their groups, any common features they can identify within the animals in the same group. These will be studied in greater detail in the rest of the module.

Ask children to choose a card from their group and complete this sentence:

This ... [name of animal] is a/an ... [name of vertebrate group].

The task

Ask children to gather the four reptile cards from their set and discuss in more detail what is the same and different about these four images.

Refer to the children's list of animals and highlight any that are reptiles. Support children with any misconceptions at this stage around reptiles as a group.

Give children access to Slideshow 2: Reptiles (the reptile 'posters'). Tell children that all reptiles lay eggs. Ask them to work in their groups to find the eggs on all four posters and discuss what is the same and what is different about the eggs. Accept answers that refer to clearly visible features such as colour or type of animal emerging.

Repeat this for other parts of the reptiles by telling the children to look at each poster and share what they notice about the following: claws; number of legs; teeth; what their body is covered in; diet.

As a class, complete these sentences:

All reptiles have ...

Most reptiles have ...

Reptiles eat ...

Pupil workbook: Complete Activity 1: What makes a reptile a reptile? on page 55.

Adaptations and support

Children may need to work with fewer cards to sort in the Getting started part of this lesson. The cards will be revisited in each lesson in the module, so more can be introduced at a later point. When studying the features of reptiles, children could choose two of the four posters.

Take it further

Connect with any members of the school community who have reptiles as pets. Invite them into school to share more about the diet and life of their reptile.

Reflect and review

Remind the children of the lesson question: **'Who's who in the animal (vertebrate) world?'** and that they have been focusing on naming vertebrates and learning the names of the five vertebrate groups. They have learnt more about reptiles in this lesson by observing their visible features closely.

Display this sentence frame, and ask children to complete it for at least two of the reptiles learned about in the lesson:

This … [name of reptile] is a reptile because … [reason from answers below].

Pupil workbook: Complete Activity 2: How do I know it is a reptile? on page 56.

Answers

Getting started:

- Reptiles: Hermann's tortoise, Nile crocodile, green iguana, corn snake
- Birds: chicken, emperor penguin, sparrow, barn owl
- Amphibians: common toad, common frog, smooth newt, red-eyed tree frog
- Fish: rainbow trout, hammerhead shark, clownfish, king salmon, common goldfish
- Mammals: horse, tiger, cow, cat, fox, zebra, giraffe, rabbit, human

The task:

The things that make reptiles distinct are: laying eggs on land and scaly skin. Many reptiles also have four legs, claws, teeth and live on land. Their diet varies between types of reptile.

Homework suggestions

Children could find out more about other reptiles they know about, including what they eat.

Assessment and evidence of learning

Children can:
- state that reptiles are one of the five vertebrate groups
- identify and name at least three reptiles
- describe and compare the structure of some reptiles
- state that all reptiles lay eggs on land and have scaly skin
- state that many reptiles have four legs, claws, teeth and live on land
- state that reptiles' diets vary between types of reptile
- provide reasons for their groupings of animals.

Lesson 2: What's so special about birds?

What children will learn and do

- Children revisit the five vertebrate groups from Lesson 1: mammals, amphibians, reptiles, birds and fish.
- They learn that the features that make birds a distinct group are: eggs, beaks, claws, wings and feathers.
- They compare different birds and their key features, looking at things that are the same and things that are not the same.
- They answer the lesson question: **'What's so special about birds?'**

You will need

- (if available) natural samples of different types of feathers for children to handle; down, wing and tail feathers are all helpful examples to support children's understanding of what makes a bird a bird
- magnifiers (optional)

Snap Science Year 1 Pupil Workbook

- pages 57–59

Snap Science Year 1 Digital subscription

- Lesson 1 Slideshow 1: Who's who
- Slideshow 1: Birds
- Slideshow 2: What do birds eat?

Make sure you have opened/printed any *Snap* resources you intend to use in this lesson.

Prepare print-outs of Slideshow 1 and Slideshow 2, with one set of each for each group of between four and six children. To reduce paper use, print the slides from Slideshow 2 on the reverse of those from Slideshow 1.

Reuse the animal cards created from slides 8–14 of Slideshow 1 from Lesson 1.

National Curriculum

Conceptual knowledge:

- identify and name a variety of common animals including [fish, amphibians, reptiles,] birds [and mammals]
- identify and name a variety of common animals that are carnivores, herbivores and omnivores
- describe and compare the structure of a variety of common animals ([fish, amphibians, reptiles,] birds [and mammals], including pets)

Working scientifically:

- observing closely, [using simple equipment]

Scientific enquiry type:

- identifying and classifying

Key vocabulary	
Tier 2 vocabulary:	**Tier 3 vocabulary:**
features	group, identify
	amphibian, bird, carnivore, diet, fish, herbivore, mammal, omnivore, reptile, vertebrate

Health and safety Please refer to CLEAPSS for Health and Safety guidance and ensure that any identified hazards are managed appropriately.

Getting started

Reuse the 26 animal cards from Lesson 1 Slideshow 1: Who's who to remind children of the five vertebrate groups – mammals, amphibians, reptiles, birds and fish – and to check what has been remembered. Ask children to work in small groups (four to six children) to sort the cards into the five groups.

Once grouped, focus on the reptiles and ask children to identify some features. The things that make reptiles distinct are: laying eggs on land and scaly skin. Many reptiles also have four legs, claws, teeth and live on land. Their diet varies between types of reptile.

Tell children that today they are going to answer the lesson question: **'What's so special about birds?'** Ask them to look at the bird cards. Ask them to talk to their group about any of these birds they have seen before. Accept birds seen in fictional settings as well as in natural habitats, zoos, wildlife reserves or as pets.

In their groups, ask children to look at what the birds in the pictures have in common. Encourage answers about how the birds look and how they move. Accept all responses centrally at this stage; these will be revisited later in the lesson.

If feathers are available for handling, share them around the class, telling children which bird they are each. Provide magnifiers so children can look at them closely. Tell them that most birds have different types of feathers within their own body, such as small, fluffy, downy feathers for warmth, strong, stiff feathers for their wings and smaller, thinner tail feathers that can help change direction during flight for some species.

Collect up the card sets.

Pupil workbook: Complete Activity 1: What do birds have in common? on page 57.

The task

Children continue working in their groups of four to six. Provide a set of bird 'posters' for each group, created using print-outs of Slideshow 1: Birds. Ask children to recognise and then name the four birds they have already seen in Lesson 1 (chicken, emperor penguin, sparrow and barn owl) then to notice the names of the six new birds (herring gull, swan, puffin, kestrel, budgerigar and rock pigeon).

Tell children that all birds lay eggs like reptiles do. Tell them to look at the eggs on each poster and discuss in their groups what is the same about the eggs and what is different.

Tell each child to select a bird poster that they are interested in. Tell them to study the images of wings, feathers, feet, beaks, eggs and hatchlings.

Call out a feature (wings, feathers, feet, beaks, eggs or hatchlings). Each time, the children are to find a partner with a different bird and compare that feature, looking for things that are the same and things that are different. Expect words related to colour, size, shape, flying or water.

Repeat this activity so children can compare their birds to at least four others.

Next, provide each group of children with print-outs of Slideshow 2: What do birds eat? Explain that these are the same birds that children have already studied in the lesson, but now children will be finding out what each type of bird eats as part of its diet. Tell children that there are scientific words which describe whether an animal eats only plants (herbivore), only other animals (carnivore) or both plants and animals (omnivore).

Ask children to choose a bird and then to find another person in the class whose bird eats one of the same things. For example, chickens and sparrows both eat grains. Repeat this at least three times to compare the diets of different birds.

Explain that the diet of a bird varies and not all birds eat the same foods. Some are herbivores, some are carnivores and some are omnivores.

Then ask children to think about what they have learnt about the similarities and differences between the features of different birds. As a class, complete these sentences:

All birds have …

Some birds have …

Pupil workbook: Complete Activity 2: What makes a bird a bird? on page 58 and Activity 3: What do birds eat? on page 59.

Adaptations and support

Some support may be needed to access the written labels.

Take it further

Ask around to learn if anyone connected to your class or school community is a keen 'twitcher' and invite them in to share local expertise and tips for bird watching.

Organise a class visit to an RSPB (Royal Society for the Protection of Birds) site or invite someone from the RSPB to visit in person or online.

Arrange for your class or school to take part in RSPB's Big Schools' Birdwatch (January annually).

Reflect and review

Remind the children of the lesson question: **'What's so special about birds?'** and that in this lesson they have been focussing on the visible features of birds by observing closely.

Display this sentence frame, and ask children to complete it for at least two of the birds learned about in the lesson:

This … [name of bird] is a bird because …

Answers

The things that make birds distinct are: eggs, beaks, claws, wings and feathers. Most birds can fly, and some can swim or spend time underwater. Their diet varies between types of bird.

The ten birds that have been chosen for this lesson are a variety of both UK native species and a range of other birds that live in different parts of the world. You may wish to replace some with ones that are more familiar to members of your class or add to the ten provided.

Information about the birds explored in the lesson:

- **Chickens** are omnivores. They eat fruits and berries, vegetables, grains, seeds and insects and other bugs. Their hatchlings are known as chicks.
- **Barn owls** are carnivores. They eat small mammals (predominantly rodents such as voles, mice and shrews) and very occasionally bats, small birds, amphibians and invertebrates. In the UK, they mainly eat voles. Owl hatchlings are known as owlets.
- **Emperor penguins** are carnivores. They eat krill, fish (particularly Antarctic silverfish) and squid. Their hatchlings are known as chicks.
- **Sparrows** are omnivores. They eat grains, seeds and insects and other bugs. Their offspring are just known as hatchlings and do not have a specific term.
- **Herring gulls** (commonly known as a seagull) are omnivores. They eat seeds, fruits, eggs, young birds, small mammals, fish and insects and other bugs. Their hatchlings are called chicks.
- **Swans** are omnivores. They eat grass, aquatic plants, insects and other bugs, vegetables (such as leafy greens) and grains. Their hatchlings are called cygnets.
- **Puffins** are carnivores. They eat fish (such as sprat, cod, herring and hake). Their hatchlings are called pufflings.

- **Kestrels**, a type of falcon, are carnivores. They eat small mammals (such as mice and shrews), small birds and insects and other bugs. Their hatchlings are sometimes known as eyas.
- **Budgerigars** are herbivores. They eat seeds, fruit and berries and vegetables. Their offspring are just known as hatchlings and do not have a specific term.
- **Rock pigeons** are omnivores. When they live away from cities, they eat grain, seeds, fruit and berries, vegetables and insects and bugs. In cities, where they are commonly found, they eat processed food from humans (such as breadcrumbs and junk food). Their hatchlings are known as squabs.

Homework suggestions

Send home a spotter guide to families, encouraging them to notice the birds in their locality and to share their findings back to school. You could also encourage them to join in the RSPB's Big Garden Birdwatch which takes place annually in January.

Assessment and evidence of learning

Children can:
- state that birds are one of the five vertebrate groups
- identify and name at least three birds
- describe and compare the structure of some birds
- state that all birds lay eggs and have beaks, claws, wings and feathers
- state that most birds can fly
- state that some birds can swim or spend time underwater
- state that birds' diets vary between types of bird
- compare different birds, stating what is the same and what is different about them.

If you are unsure if children are secure in their knowledge about the remaining three vertebrate groups (amphibians, fish and mammals), these will be studied in more depth within the rest of the module.

Lesson 3: What makes an amphibian an amphibian?

What children will learn and do

- Children revisit the five vertebrate groups from Lessons 1 and 2: mammals, amphibians, reptiles, birds and fish.

- They learn that the things that make amphibians a distinct group are: they lay eggs, they live on land and in water and their diet changes with their stage of life.

- They compare different amphibians and their key features, looking at things that are the same and things that are not the same.

- They answer the lesson question: **'What makes an amphibian an amphibian?'**

You will need

- first-hand opportunity to observe the life cycle of a common frog (optional)

Snap Science Year 1 Pupil Workbook

- pages 60–62

Snap Science Year 1 Digital subscription

- Lesson 1 Slideshow 1: Who's who
- Slideshow 1: The stages of a frog's life
- Slideshow 2: Amphibians

Make sure you have opened/printed any *Snap* resources you intend to use in this lesson.

Prepare printouts of Slideshow 2, with one set for each group of between four and six children.

Reuse the animal cards created from slides 8–14 of Slideshow 1 from Lesson 1.

National Curriculum

Conceptual knowledge:

- identify and name a variety of common animals including [fish,] amphibians, [reptiles, birds and mammals]

- identify and name a variety of common animals that are carnivores, herbivores and omnivores

- describe and compare the structure of a variety of common animals ([fish,] amphibians, [reptiles, birds and mammals,] including pets)

Working scientifically:

- observing closely, [using simple equipment]

Key vocabulary	
Tier 2 vocabulary: features	**Tier 3 vocabulary:** group amphibian, bird, carnivore, diet, fish, herbivore, identify, mammal, reptile, vertebrate

Health and safety Please refer to CLEAPSS for Health and Safety guidance and ensure that any identified hazards are managed appropriately.

If the frog lifecycle is being studied first-hand, please ensure the animals are cared for and passed on appropriately.

Getting started

Reuse the 26 animal cards from Lesson 1 Slideshow 1: Who's who to remind children of the five vertebrate groups: mammals, amphibians, reptiles, birds and fish. As in Lessons 1 and 2, children should work in groups of four to six. Ask them to group and name the animals on the cards. Children should be more familiar with the animals on the cards now, so should be able to group them more quickly at this stage.

Once the cards are grouped, ask children to identify the reptiles and birds groups from Lessons 1 and 2 and to talk to their group about what makes a bird a bird and a reptile a reptile.

Tell children that today they are going to answer the lesson question: **'What makes an amphibian an amphibian?'** Ask them to focus on the amphibian cards and talk to their group about any of these amphibians they have seen before. Accept amphibians seen in fictional settings as well as in natural habitats, zoos, wildlife reserves or as pets.

In their groups, ask children to look at what the amphibians in the pictures have in common. Accept all responses centrally at this stage; these will be revisited later in the lesson.

Present Slideshow 1: The stages of a frog's life. Show the slides several times, pointing out that this is the same animal, growing up and changing.

If it is possible for children to study the stages of life of a frog first-hand by visiting a pond, draw on their experiences of where the frogs are in their growth and what will happen in the future. Remember, this is not a life cycle lesson (this will be studied in Year 5, Module 4 Plant and animal life cycles, Lesson 5), it is just a way of making it clear that what makes an amphibian an amphibian is the changes that happen during their different stages of life.

Collect up the sets of cards, except for the four amphibian cards (common toad, common frog, smooth newt and red-eyed tree frog).

Pupil workbook: Complete Activity 1: What do amphibians have in common? on page 60.

The task

Using the four amphibian cards, ask children to talk in groups of four about what is the same about these animals and what is different, using what they can see on the cards. Collect any thoughts centrally and note any questions they have at this stage.

Provide printouts of the amphibian 'posters' from Slideshow 2: Amphibians (one set per group of four children). Also display Slideshow 2: Amphibians on a screen so you can flick between the posters when you are collecting responses.

Explain that one of the things that makes an amphibian an amphibian is that they change during their life, starting on or in the water and ending as adults living near water but mainly on land. Also explain that they can swim and breathe underwater when they are young and develop lungs for breathing air on land as they grow up. Tell children that this is unique to this type of vertebrate.

Also, draw children's attention to the way the diet of an amphibian can change at different stages of its life. For example, common frogs are herbivores when they are tadpoles, but become carnivores when they reach the froglet stage.

Ask each child to choose one of the four amphibian 'posters' and use it to find out about that amphibian. Then ask them to compare their findings with one other person in their group.

Once both children have shared, ask them to share as a group of four, noticing similarities and differences.

You may wish to provide a speaking frame to support this activity, such as: 'My amphibian is a … [name of amphibian] and it is the same as/different to a … [another amphibian] because they both/neither of them … [characteristic such as: start life underwater as a tadpole]. Some children may be able to make connections with more than two amphibians in their sentences.

After a suitable period of time, collect responses centrally, showing the amphibians on the screen at the time to highlight the similarities and differences.

Draw attention to the list made earlier in the lesson, of things children thought the amphibians in the pictures had in common (based on the cards from Lesson 1). It is likely they noticed features such as skin colour or body shape. Now that they understand the importance of the changing stages of life, children should better understand the differences between different amphibians.

Pupil workbook: Complete Activity 2: Life stages of amphibians on page 61 and Activity 3: The Common toad on page 62.

Adaptations and support

Reading support might be required for some children when using Slideshow 2: Amphibians.

Take it further

You could connect with your local nature reserve for a visit as a class, or invite an expert to share their knowledge of amphibians with your class in person or online.

Reflect and review

Remind the children of the lesson question: **'What makes an amphibian an amphibian?'** and that in this lesson they have been focusing on the features of amphibians by looking at their changing stages of life.

Display this sentence frame, and ask children to complete it for at least two of the amphibians learned about in the lesson:

This … [name of amphibian] is an amphibian because …

Answers

Getting started:

- The things that make reptiles distinct are: laying eggs on land and scaly skin. Many reptiles also have four legs, claws, teeth and live on land. Their diet varies between types of reptile.
- The things that make birds distinct are: eggs, beaks, claws, wings and feathers. Most birds can fly, some can swim or spend time underwater. Their diet varies between types of bird.

When sharing Slideshow 1: The stages of a frog's life, here is some further information about each stage of life for a **common frog**:

- When it is in egg form, it is known as spawn.
- Once hatched, it is known as a tadpole.
- Once it has grown enough to be able to live on land, it is known as a froglet.
- Once fully grown, it is known as a frog (in this case, the common frog)

This information is the same for all amphibians; it is the names of the stages that vary slightly between different species.

The task:

The things that make amphibians distinct are: they lay eggs, they live on land and in water and their diet changes with their changing stages of life.

Amphibians' breathing changes with their changing stages of life. (This point is helpful for you as a teacher to understand, but it is not essential learning for the children.)

Information about the amphibians studied in this lesson:

- **Common toad** – the adult female common toad lays large chains of eggs, known as spawn. When they first hatch, the tadpoles can swim, breathe in water and are herbivores. Once they are toadlets, they change from gills to air-breathing lungs, and they become carnivorous. Once they reach adulthood, they remain carnivorous. Adult toads tend to walk rather than hop and

---

are characterised by their broad, squat bodies and warty skin. They tend to live away from the water as adults and hibernate in the winter

- **Common frog** – unlike toads, the adult female common frog lays large clumps of eggs, known as spawn, in spring (usually in February or March in the UK). Like toads, when they first hatch, the tadpoles can swim, breathe in water and are herbivores. Once they are froglets, they change from gills to air-breathing lungs, and they become carnivorous. Once they reach adulthood, they can live on land and in water, and remain carnivorous.
- **Smooth newt** – the adult female smooth newt lays their individual eggs, known as spawn, on water plants. The larvae (also known as newt tadpoles) hatch soon after. They can swim and breathe in the water and are herbivores. The newtlets (or efts) develop front legs first, unlike frogs and toads. At this stage, they can breathe air, are now carnivorous and move to live more on land. Adult smooth newts will often live in compost heaps or buried in the mud during winter and can be found sheltering under rocks and paving slabs in the late summer and autumn.
- **Red-eyed tree frog** – the stages of life of a tree frog vary greatly from species to species and so the points noted here are just about this particular species, which is common in Mexico, Guatemala and Honduras. The adult female red-eyed tree frog lays her eggs on leaves overhanging water. When the tadpoles hatch, they drop into the water. Like all the other amphibians studied, the tadpoles can swim and breathe underwater. But unlike the other amphibians, they are carnivores at this stage and feed on insects. They then develop into froglets and move into the trees to live. As they become adults, they develop flashes of blue and yellow on the sides of their green bodies, red or orange feet and big red eyes.

Homework suggestions

If children live near a pond or stream, or have the opportunity to visit somewhere like an RSPB site, they could see if they can spot any signs of amphibians nearby such as spawn in clumps or strings.

Assessment and evidence of learning

Children can:
- state that amphibians are one of the five vertebrate groups
- identify and name at least two amphibians
- state that all amphibians lay eggs and live on land and in water
- state that amphibians' diets change with their changing stages of life
- compare different amphibians, stating what is the same and what is different about them.

If you are unsure if children are secure in their knowledge about the remaining two vertebrate groups (fish and mammals), these will be studied in more depth within the rest of the module.

Lesson 4: Do fish have fingers?

What children will learn and do

- Children revisit the five vertebrate groups from Lessons 1–3: mammals, amphibians, reptiles, birds and fish.

- They learn that the things that make fish a distinct group are: they lay eggs, they have gills to help them breathe underwater, they have fins and a tail to help them swim and most fish have scales to protect them.

- They observe fish closely, looking for their key features including eyes, tail, fins, scales, teeth, mouth and gills.

- They answer the lesson question: **'Do fish have fingers?'**

You will need

- a selection of between three and five varieties of fresh whole fish from your local fishmongers, market or supermarket (choose from mackerel, rainbow trout, hake, sea bass, perch or plaice if possible)

- trays of ice (one per fish)

- magnifiers (ideally one per child)

- paper towels or dishcloths to wipe the tables afterwards

Prepare the trays of fish before the lesson and leave out of sight but covered.

If using the Snap Science Year 1 Pupil Workbook you may not require all of the resource sheets below.

Snap Science Year 1 Pupil Workbook

- pages 63–65

Snap Science Year 1 Digital subscription

- Lesson 1 Slideshow 1: Who's who
- Video 1: What is a fish?
- Slideshow 1: Different fish
- Resource sheet 1: Key fish vocabulary
- Resource sheet 2: Detailed drawings of fish

Make sure you have opened/printed any *Snap* resources you intend to use in this lesson.

You may wish to print Slideshow 1 for closer inspection if fresh whole fish are not available.

Prepare sets of vocabulary cards using Resource sheet 1: Key fish vocabulary, with one set of cards for each group of between four and six children.

Reuse the animal cards created from slides 8–14 of Slideshow 1 from Lesson 1.

National Curriculum

Conceptual knowledge:

- identify and name a variety of common animals including fish, [amphibians, reptiles, birds and mammals]

- identify and name a variety of common animals that are carnivores, herbivores and omnivores

- describe and compare the structure of a variety of common animals (fish, [amphibians, reptiles, birds and mammals,] including pets)

Working scientifically:

- observing closely, using simple equipment

Key vocabulary	
Tier 2 vocabulary:	**Tier 3 vocabulary:**
features, structure	group, identify
	amphibian, bird, diet, fish, mammal, reptile, vertebrate

Health and safety Please refer to CLEAPSS for Health and Safety guidance and ensure that any identified hazards are managed appropriately.

Before children begin handling fresh fish, ensure they all understand the importance of not touching their own mouths, eyes, etc. until their hands have been thoroughly washed.

Getting started

Ask each child to draw a picture of a fish. Give minimal guidance. Collect the drawings and save them for later in the lesson.

Reuse the 26 animal cards from Lesson 1 Slideshow 1: Who's who to remind children of the five vertebrate groups: mammals, amphibians, reptiles, birds and fish. Ask them to group and name the animals on the cards.

Once the cards are grouped, ask children to identify the reptiles, birds and amphibians groups from Lessons 1, 2 and 3 and to talk to their group about what makes a bird, a reptile and an amphibian distinct from other vertebrates. Ask children to notice anything that all three of these vertebrate groups have in common. Support them to notice that all three lay eggs.

Collect all the cards that are not fish.

Tell children that today they are going to answer the lesson question: **'Do fish have fingers?'** Ask children to focus on the fish cards and talk to their group about any of the fish they have seen before. Accept fish seen in fictional settings as well as in natural habitats, zoos, wildlife reserves or as pets.

In their groups, ask children to look at features that the fish group have in common. Record their responses centrally. Note any questions that arise and return to them later in the lesson.

Play Video 1: What is a fish? and help children to notice that the structure of a fish is what they all have in common (eyes, mouth, gills, fins and a tail) and that most fish have scales. Repeat the video as required.

Collect up the cards.

Pupil workbook: Complete Activity 1: What do fish have in common? on page 63.

The task

Display Slideshow 1: Different fish. Share each slide, explaining that these are fish that we (humans) commonly eat and that the photos show the fish in their natural habitat (sea, river, stream, etc.) as well as how they might look on the fish counter in a shop.

Taking each word in turn and looking at each slide again, ask children if they can identify the eyes, mouth, teeth, scales, gills, fins or tail. It is likely that you will need to explain what gills, fins and scales are, and it is unlikely that children will be able to identify teeth or perhaps scales on some of the photos.

Once you are sure children are familiar with identifying those parts on the photos, split them into groups of between three and six. Provide each group with a tray containing ice and one fish, hand lenses and a pre-prepared set of vocabulary cards created using Resource sheet 1: Key fish vocabulary. Ask children to explore the fish in front of them and add all the labels they can to the fish by placing them on the body parts. Encourage children to lift the fish, open out the fins and tail, open the gills and put their finger inside the fish's mouth. The discovery of teeth on some species may surprise.

After a suitable period, ask them to remove all the labels, then move around the room to a different fish so they can repeat for another species. Do this as many times as appropriate depending on time and number of species available to explore.

If appropriate, on the final rotation, provide each child with a copy of Resource sheet 2: Detailed drawings of fish. Tell them to choose three parts of the fish to focus on and draw them carefully. They can then compare their drawings with someone in another group and discuss what is similar and what is different about their species.

Refer back to any questions children had earlier in the lesson that have not yet been addressed.

Pupil workbook: Complete Activity 2: Parts of a fish on page 64 and Activity 3: What do fish eat? On page 65.

Adaptations and support

Some children may be anxious about touching the fish, or uncomfortable with the smell. Ensure you are aware of any children who do not eat fish and do not expect children to touch the fish if they don't want to. Encourage them to watch others place the labels but let them know they can join in at any stage if they want to.

Take it further

Find out if anyone connected with your class keeps either tropical or freshwater fish in a tank or pond. Invite them to come and speak to the class and perhaps share a video of their fish and help the children to notice their eyes, mouth, gills, fins and tail.

Reflect and review

Ask the lesson question: **'Do fish have fingers?'** and ask them to share a reason for their answer. Expect responses such as: 'Fish do not have fingers as they do not need to pick up things. They have fins to help them swim instead.'

Hand the drawings back to the children that they did at the start of the lesson and ask them how would they draw their fish any differently now they have learned more about them? If time allows, ask them to draw a final labelled diagram of a fish to compare.

Answers

Getting started:

- The things that make reptiles distinct are: laying eggs on land and scaly skin. Many reptiles also have four legs, claws, teeth and live on land. Their diet varies between types of reptile.
- The things that make birds distinct are: eggs, beaks, claws, wings and feathers. Most birds can fly, some can swim or spend time underwater. Their diet varies between types of bird.
- The things that make amphibians distinct are: they lay eggs, they live on land and in water and their diet changes with their changing stages of life.

The five fish on the cards from Lesson 1 Slideshow 1: Who's who have been selected for the range of habitat, shape, size and diet. On the whole, fish eat other smaller fish and are carnivores. There are some exceptions used here.

- **Rainbow trout** – a river fish native to the rivers and lakes of northwest America. They can be found in UK rivers and canals. They are carnivorous, eating mainly insects and other smaller fish.
- **Clown fish** – a tropical sea fish found in the warm waters of the Red Sea and Pacific Ocean, sheltered In lagoons and reefs. They are omnivores, eating algae and other small invertebrates.
- **Hammerhead shark** – a sea fish living alone along the coastal areas of the Atlantic, Pacific and Indian Oceans and the Mediterranean Sea. They are carnivores and eat other larger fish plus rays, skates, squid, lobsters and eels.

- **King salmon** – this species is a sea fish; other species of salmon live in rivers. They are native to the northwest coast of North America and northeast Asia. They are carnivores and eat other smaller fish including krill, shrimp, squid and herring.
- **Common goldfish** – in their natural habitat, they live in still bodies of water such as rivers, lakes, ponds and streams. They are omnivores and eat insects, plants and crustaceans.

The task:

The six fish in Slideshow 1: Different fish for this lesson have been chosen as they are likely to be the species you can get from your local fish counter to explore first-hand. They range from sea to river fish, those that live on the seabed to tiny fish in lakes and streams. Try to get a range of fish for the children to look at.

- **Mackerel** – a sea fish. They are carnivorous and eat smaller fish, krill, shrimp and squid.
- **Rainbow trout** – (see information above).
- **Hake** – a sea fish. They are carnivorous and eat mackerel, herring, squid and any other smaller fish they come across.
- **Sea bass** – a sea fish. They are carnivorous and feed mainly on shrimp and molluscs plus squid and other smaller fish.
- **Perch** – a freshwater fish. They are carnivorous and invertebrates and small fish.
- **Plaice** – a sea fish. They are carnivorous and feed on shellfish like cockles and razor clams and also worms and sand eels.

Homework suggestions

Next time they are in a shop that sells whole fish, children could name the parts of the fish they see and notice differences and similarities between them.

Assessment and evidence of learning

Children can:
- state that fish are one of the five vertebrate groups
- identify and name at least four different fish
- state that all fish lay eggs and have eyes, mouth, gills, fins and tail
- state that some fish have scales
- compare the structure of different fish, stating what is the same and what is different about them
- use magnifiers correctly
- identify what is missing from the picture of a fish they drew at the start of the lesson.

If you are unsure if children are secure in their knowledge about the remaining vertebrate group (mammals), this will be studied in the remaining lesson.

Lesson 5: Are humans mammals?

What children will learn and do

- Children learn that the things that make mammals a distinct group are: they have hair/fur, give birth to live young, produce milk for offspring, nurture offspring, look like a younger version of their parents and have a range of movement.
- They learn that humans are mammals and compare different mammals and their offspring.
- They revisit the five vertebrate groups from all previous lessons in the module to name them, compare their structures and notice their diets.
- They answer the lesson question: **'Are humans mammals?'**

You will need

- sets of three sorting hoops for each group of four to six children (these could be drawn on the playground, on tables or on paper as required)

Snap Science Year 1 Pupil Workbook

- pages 66–68

Snap Science Year 1 Digital subscription

- Lesson 1 Slideshow 1: Who's who?
- Slideshow 1: Who are their parents?
- Slideshow 2: Herbivores, omnivores, carnivores
- Snapshot activity 1: Name that animal!
- Snapshot activity 2: Who eats what?
- Snapshot activity 3: Describe and compare

Make sure you have opened/printed any *Snap* resources you intend to use in this lesson.

Reuse the animal cards created from slides 8–14 of Slideshow 1 from Lesson 1.

National Curriculum

Conceptual knowledge:

- identify and name a variety of common animals including fish, amphibians, reptiles, birds and mammals
- identify and name a variety of common animals that are carnivores, herbivores and omnivores
- describe and compare the structure of a variety of common animals (fish, amphibians, reptiles, birds and mammals, including pets)

Working scientifically:

- observing closely, using simple equipment
- using their observations and ideas to suggest answers to questions

Key vocabulary	
Tier 2 vocabulary:	**Tier 3 vocabulary:**
features	group, identify
	amphibian, bird, carnivore, classify, diet, fish, herbivore, mammal, omnivore, reptile, vertebrate

Health and safety Please refer to CLEAPSS for Health and Safety guidance and ensure that any identified hazards are managed appropriately.

Getting started

Reuse the 26 animal cards from Lesson 1 Slideshow 1: Who's who. Give a set of cards to each group of four to six children. Ask them to select the animals they have not yet learnt more about in the other lessons and put the rest of the pack to one side. Do not use the word mammal just yet. They may need help to identify some of the mammals pictured: horse, tiger, cow, cat, fox, zebra, giraffe, rabbit and human. Ensure they can name them all.

Tell them to take out the human card and put it face down, then spread the rest of the animals face up in front of them.

Ask children if they can remember what this group of animals is called and check that everyone knows they are mammals. Tell them the features that make mammals distinct one at a time: have hair/fur covering their bodies; give birth to live young; produce milk for their offspring; nurture their offspring; look like a younger version of their parents; have a range of movement. See if children can spot any of these features in the photos, or can you tell you about them from existing knowledge. Expect them to be able to see that the mammals have hair or fur in the pictures, but to be less certain about the other features at this stage.

Tell children that today they are going to answer the lesson question: **'Are humans mammals?'** Ask them to add the human card to the set. Repeat the list of features and ask children to notice if humans have any of these.

Display Slideshow 1: Who are their parents? Before showing each slide, ask children if they know the name of the offspring or the adult female of each species.

Now repeat the list of features and see if children are able to see more of these features now. Collect any responses and questions that arise and ensure you allow time to revisit them later in the lesson.

Once you are sure that the children know the features that all mammals, including humans, have in common, move on.

Pupil workbook: Complete Activity 1: What is a mammal? on page 66.

The task

Ensure each group of four to six children has a full set of the 26 animal cards from Lesson 1 Slideshow 1: Who's who. Ask them to group them into the five vertebrate groups one more time (fish, amphibians, reptiles, birds and mammals). Expect them to do this confidently and quickly at this stage.

Now ask each group to consider what the diet of each animal is. Out of the 26 animals, expect them to know about the diet of at least ten of them and at least two from each vertebrate group, drawing on prior learning and existing knowledge. They do not need to use the words herbivore, omnivore and carnivore at this point, but they should be able to describe what the animal eats.

Tell them to group animals they know the diet of together. Display a speaking frame to support children's discussions: I have put … [name of animal] and … [name of other animal] together because they both eat … [name of food].

Display Slideshow 2: Herbivores, omnivores, carnivores. Show Slide 1 and tell children that scientists use the word 'carnivore' to group together animals that only eat meat, 'herbivore' to group together animals that only eat plants, and 'omnivore' to group together animals that eat both plants and meat. Explain that this is another way to group animals, just like they have been doing for the whole of this module into vertebrate groups.

Ask them to work together as a group to try and classify some of the animals (using the 26 animal cards) into those three groups. They should aim to classify at least ten of them from across a range of the vertebrate groups.

Slides 2–4 show all 26 animals grouped according to their diet. Note that common frog, common toad and smooth newt appear on two slides as their diet changes with their life stage. Display these slides for children to compare and discuss, allowing time to address any questions or existing conceptions at this stage that still need clarity.

Pupil workbook: Complete Activity 2: Carnivores, herbivores and omnivores on page 67.

Adaptations and support

Provide support for children to identify the diet of different animals through questions prompting them to recall where the different types of animal live and what food might grow or live there.

Take it further

A visit to a local wildlife park, zoo or farm would offer lots of opportunities to learn about a wider range of mammals and ideally see their young at the same time. Some mobile farms come into school and offer this experience first-hand.

The children could find out about the diet of other mammals they know and the name of the offspring and the adult female of the species.

Reflect and review

Remind the children of the lesson question: **'Are humans mammals?'** and that in this lesson they have been focusing on the features and offspring of mammals.

Ask children to write a sentence to explain why a human is a mammal. Then ask them to write a second sentence comparing a human to another mammal. Use these sentence frames for support:

A human is a mammal because …

This is a … [other mammal]. It is a mammal, like a human, because they both …

Pupil workbook: Complete Activity 3: This is a mammal because… on page 68.

Answers

Getting started:

The things that make mammals distinct are: they have hair/fur, give birth to live young, produce milk for offspring, nurture offspring, look like a younger version of their parents and have a range of movement.

Diet of mammals featured in Slideshow 1: Who are their parents:

- **horse** – herbivore
- **tiger** – carnivore
- **cow** – herbivore
- **cat** – carnivore (although cats will eat other foods when kept as pets, they are 'obligate carnivores', which means they are reliant on meat for their nutrition)
- **fox** – omnivore
- **zebra** – herbivore
- **giraffe** – herbivore
- **rabbit** – herbivore
- **human** – omnivore (but early humans were herbivores)

Adult female and offspring names for each mammal featured in Slideshow 1: Who are their parents:

- **horse** – mare and foal
- **tiger** – tigress and cub
- **cow** – cow and calf
- **cat** – queen and kitten
- **fox** – vixen and pup, cub or kit
- **zebra** – mare and foal
- **giraffe** – cow and calf

- **rabbit** – doe and kit
- **human** – woman and baby

Note that children may notice that some words for the adult female or the offspring are the same for more than one animal. You can tell them that this is because scientists further group mammals into smaller groups and often the same names are used. For example, large placental mammals such as elephant, cow, giraffe and whale all have calves. It is not necessary for children in Year 1 to learn or understand this, but it may help you respond to any questions that arise during this lesson.

Homework suggestions

Ask children to think about any pets they, or family members have. To which of the five vertebrate groups do they belong? Does anyone have a pet which is not a vertebrate?

Assessment and evidence of learning

Children can:

- state that mammals are one of the five vertebrate groups
- identify and name at least four mammals
- state that all mammals have hair/fur, give birth to live young, produce milk for offspring, nurture their offspring, look like younger version of their parents and have a range of movement
- compare different mammals, stating what is the same and what is different about them
- identify and name some animals that are herbivores, omnivores and carnivores
- group animals into the five vertebrate groups.

If you are unsure if a child can identify and name a variety of common animals including fish, amphibians, reptiles, birds and mammals, you can use the Snapshot activity: Name that animal!

If you are unsure if a child can identify and name a variety of common animals that are carnivores, herbivores and omnivores, you can use the Snapshot activity: Who eats what?

If you are unsure if a child can describe and compare the structure of a variety of common animals (fish, amphibians, reptiles, birds and mammals, including pets), you can use the Snapshot activity: Describe and compare.

Module 6: Identifying plants and their parts

Lesson 1: What wild and garden plants can we find around our school?

What children will learn and do

- Children learn that plants can be placed into groups depending on whether they are wild or garden plants.
- They learn the names of a range of common wild and garden plants.
- They use a guide to identify the names of some common plants.
- They answer the lesson question: **'What wild and garden plants can we find around our school?'**

You will need

- access to a variety of garden plants (such as petunias, begonias, busy lizzies, fuchsias, lilies, daffodils and tulips) in the school grounds (borders or containers) or in a local community garden, allotment or park
- access to a variety of wild plants (such as thistles, bluebells, foxgloves, daisies, buttercups, dandelions and nettles) growing in school grounds or accessible local sites (identify these in advance so that you can guide children's searches)
- magnifiers (optional)
- cameras (optional)

If using the Snap Science Year 1 Pupil Workbook you may not require the resource sheet below.

Snap Science Year 1 Pupil Workbook

- pages 69–70

Snap Science Year 1 Digital subscription

- Slideshow 1: Garden plants and wild plants
- Resource sheet 1: Identification guide: garden plants and wild plants

Make sure you have opened/printed any *Snap* resources you intend to use in this lesson.

National Curriculum

Conceptual knowledge:

- identify and name a variety of common wild and garden plants, including deciduous and evergreen trees

Working scientifically:

- observing closely using simple equipment
- identifying and classifying

Scientific enquiry type:

- Identifying and classifying

Key vocabulary	
Tier 2 vocabulary:	**Tier 3 vocabulary:**
similar	group, identify
adjectives to describe colour, shape, size, texture and smell	flower, leaf, plant, roots, stem

Health and safety Please refer to CLEAPSS for Health and Safety guidance and ensure that any identified hazards are managed appropriately.

Getting started

Ask children to draw a plant that they have seen growing, either at home, on their walk to school, in the local park or in the school grounds. Ask them to label any parts of their plant that they can name. Ask: How are your drawings similar? Do they all have leaves? Are they the same shape? Do any have flowers? Do they have stems? Do any drawings show roots? Are the plants in a pot, a garden or somewhere else? Do you know the name of the plant that you have drawn?

Explain that plants can be grouped (split into different groups) depending on whether they are growing wild (wild plants) or have been planted by people (garden plants), and that today children are going to answer the lesson question: **'What wild and garden plants can we find around our school?'**

Present Slideshow 1: Garden plants and wild plants, slides 1–4 (garden plants). Ask children if they know what gardeners do to grow garden plants. At this stage, accept sensible suggestions such as planting, watering and weeding, as children will learn about this in greater detail when they grow their own garden plant.

Ask: Which garden plant do you think has the most interesting name? Why do you think it is called that? What do you notice about where the garden plants are growing?

Then show sides 5–8 (wild plants). Ask children what they notice about where the wild plants are growing and compare this with where the garden plants are growing.

Ask: Which wild plant do you think has the most interesting name? Why do you think it is called that?

It is sufficient for children to know that many common wild plants grow easily in places where gardeners do not want them and are called 'weeds'.

Stop presenting Slideshow 1: Garden plants and wild plants. Ask children to think about all the plants they have seen in the lesson so far (both garden and wild). Ask whether they can remember the names of the plants.

Pupil workbook: Complete Activity 1: Identifying wild and garden plants on page 69.

The task

Take children to a planted area and point to and name the different garden plants. Remind them of the plant names throughout the lesson and suggest ways to remember them. Then point out examples of common wild plants. Name them one by one, focusing on the most common varieties they have already seen on the slides.

Using Resource sheet 1: Identification guide: garden plants and wild plants, children should identify at least one wild and one garden plant. They can either take photographs or draw them. They should add its name, where it is growing and whether it is a wild or garden plant. Children could label the stem, leaves and flowers (if the plants have them), but learning the names of the parts of the plants is a focus for future lessons. These recordings should be kept as they will be used in Lesson 2.

Pupil workbook: Complete Activity 2: Wild or garden plants? on page 70.

Adaptations and support

Some children could photograph the plants and use apps which allow them to be labelled easily.

Take it further

Ask children whether they agree with this statement: 'Some gardeners think that some wild plants such as the daisy and the buttercup are weeds and that they should be dug up if they are growing in a lawn.'

Reflect and review

Remind children of today's lesson question: **'What wild and garden plants can we find around our school?'** and that in this lesson they have been focussing on naming plants. They have learnt that some plants grow wild without the help of gardeners, while others are deliberately planted and looked after and these are called garden plants. They have used identification guides to name the plants.

Display this sentence frame: 'This name of this plant is ___ and it is a (garden/wild) plant because ___'.

Ask children to complete this sentence for each of the two plants they identified in the school grounds.

Then return to Slideshow 1: Garden plants and wild plants and show slides 9–16. Ask children to complete the sentence above (verbally) for the plants on these slides.

Answers

A plant is usually called a garden plant if it has been grown by a gardener. They can be found in pots and flower borders. If found in fields, they tend to be planted in rows.

A plant is usually called a wild plant if it has not been planted by a gardener. These can be found in places such as overgrown fields, within hedgerows and in cracks of the pavement.

Plants pictured in Slideshow 1: Garden plants and wild plants:

- garden plants (slides 1–4): pansy, geranium, busy lizzie, petunia, fuchsia, lily, daffodil, tulip
- wild plants (slides 5–8): buttercup, stinging nettle, thistle, poppy, dandelion, daisy, cornflower, bluebell.

Homework suggestions

Children could look for the plants that they have learnt about in their lesson in places other than the school grounds.

Assessment and evidence of learning

Children can:
- state that plants can be grouped into wild plants and garden plants
- name a variety of common wild and garden plants they have seen
- explain why they think a plant is a wild plant or a garden plant
- identify at least one wild and one garden plant from the school grounds.

SNAP SCIENCE
GET YOUR TEETH INTO IT!
2nd EDITION

Lesson 2: What parts of a plant grow above the ground?

What children will learn and do

- Children learn that many plants have stems, leaves and flowers.
- They learn that these parts of the plant grow above the ground.
- They label stems, leaves and flowers on pictures of plants.
- They compare stems, leaves and flowers on different plants.
- They answer the lesson question: **'What parts of a plant grow above the ground?'**

You will need

- children's recordings of plants from the previous lesson
- a range of plant catalogues
- leaves, stems and flowers from some of the plants studied in the previous lesson (such as dandelions, daisies and buttercups); these can be collected in advance by the teacher or the children from the school grounds using their identification guides
- magnifiers

If using the Snap Science Year 1 Pupil Workbook you may not require the resource sheet below.

Snap Science Year 1 Pupil Workbook

- page 71

Snap Science Year 1 Digital subscription

- Slideshow 1: Can you name these plants?
- Resource sheet 1: Stems, leaves and flowers (optional)

Make sure you have opened/printed any *Snap* resources you intend to use in this lesson.

National Curriculum

Conceptual knowledge:

- identify and describe the basic structure of a variety of common flowering plants, including trees

Working scientifically:

- observing closely, using simple equipment

Key vocabulary	
Tier 2 vocabulary:	**Tier 3 vocabulary:**
compare, describe, different, similar, texture	identify
adjectives to describe colour, shape, size, texture and smell	flower, leaf, plant, stem

Health and safety Please refer to CLEAPSS for Health and Safety guidance and ensure that any identified hazards are managed appropriately.

Getting started

Remind children of the plants they studied in the previous lesson. Let them know that they will be looking at these and other plants to answer the lesson question: **'What parts of a plant grow above the ground?'**

Tell children to look at their recordings of plants from the previous lesson. Ask them to show their plant's stems, flowers and leaves, reminding them that these are the parts of a plant which grow above the ground.

Present Slideshow 1: Can you name these plants? Ask children if they can name some of the plants that they studied in the previous lesson, as an opportunity to retrieve previous learning.

Ask children to point to the stems, flowers and leaves on each of the plants. Pay particular attention to the flowers of the stinging nettle which are small and white. Tell children that not all flowers are large and pretty.

Explain that flowers start off as buds before they open up. Present the slideshow again and ask children to identify the plants that have flower buds.

(Note: what look like individual petals on the dandelion and daisy are tiny individual flowers called florets. At this stage it is appropriate for them to be referred to as petals. The lines in a leaf are called veins. The functions of the plant parts do not need to be learnt as this will be covered in future topics.)

Choose two plants from the slideshow and model how you can compare the different plant parts. Ask children what is the same and what is different about the leaves, stems and flowers.

The task

Provide plant catalogues and ask children to cut out pictures of different plants and label the flowers (and flower buds if present), leaves and stems on each photograph.

Explain to children how they will use the real plants provided for the following activity. Daisies, dandelions and buttercups are good plants for children to study because of their availability. Ask children to compare the leaves, stems and flowers of at least two different plants. Tell them to describe each plant's features and look for what is similar and what is different. Ask children to concentrate on features such as colour, texture, size, shape and number of petals. They can use magnifiers. Remind them how they used these to look carefully at materials earlier in the year.

If real plants are not available, children can undertake this activity using the photographs provided on Resource sheet 1: Stems, leaves and flowers.

Pupil workbook: Complete Activity 1: Comparing plant parts on page 71.

Adaptations and support

Provide pre-cut-out photographs from the plant catalogues, and/or plant part labels.

Take it further

Children compare a wider range of plants.

Reflect and review

Remind children of the lesson question: **'What parts of a plant grow above the ground?'** and that they have been focusing on stems, leaves and flowers and how they are different in different plants.

Ask children to compare their observations with other members of the class using the following structure:

The leaf/stem/flower of my [name of first flower] is similar to the leaf/stem/flower of my [name of second flower] because it …

The leaf/stem/flower of my [name of first flower] is different from the leaf/stem/flower of my [name of second flower] because it …

Encourage reference to colour, texture, size, shape and number of petals.

Ask children what they did to help them answer the lesson question. Confirm that they looked closely at the plants and noticed which parts they all had above the ground. This is how scientists work, observing closely and systematically, and looking for similarities.

End by saying that children will be looking at what part of the plant grows under the ground in the next lesson.

Answers

In Slideshow 1: Can you name these plants, the names of the plants on slides 1–4 can be found on slides 5–8 (dandelion, daisy, poppy, pansy, petunia, daffodil, nettle, fuchsia).

Some of the flowers are in bud so they cannot be seen fully. Flower buds can be found in the following photographs: daisy, poppy, petunia and fuchsia.

Homework suggestions

Ask children to identify their favourite plant and give reasons for their choice. These plants could be found on their way home from school, in the school grounds, in local parks or in personal gardens.

Assessment and evidence of learning

Children can:
- state that the parts of a plant found above the ground are the leaves, stems and flowers
- label different plant parts as stems, flowers, flower buds and leaves
- compare a plant part of one plant with another, referring to colour, texture, size, shape and number of petals.

Lesson 3: What part of a plant grows under the ground?

What children will learn and do

- Children learn that the part of the plant that grows under the ground is the roots.
- They learn that there are two types of roots: tap roots and branching roots.
- They observe roots on living plants to notice similarities between different types of roots.
- They answer the lesson question: **'What part of a plant grows under the ground?'**

You will need

- potted plants with branching roots, such as begonias, busy lizzies and pansies
- magnifiers
- larger pots than the potted plants have come in
- soil
- root vegetables such as carrots, beetroot, celeriac, daikon or radishes
- a prepared piece of land for planting (optional)
- trowels for digging (optional)
- carrot tops prepared by the teacher, about 2 cm in depth (optional)

If you grow plants for use in the lesson, you should:

- Use peat-free compost. Peatlands are the world's largest carbon store on land. They also provide important ecosystems for plants and animals and act like sponges, which reduces the risk of flooding. Therefore it is important not to use a peat-based compost for gardening.
- For plant pots, choose either biodegradable pots, or pots made from old newspapers, wood, stone, metal, terracotta or recycled plastic.

Snap Science Year 1 Pupil Workbook

- Pages 72–73

Snap Science Year 1 Digital subscription

- Slideshow 1: Roots

Make sure you have opened/printed any *Snap* resources you intend to use in this lesson.

National Curriculum

Conceptual knowledge:

- identify and describe the basic structure of a variety of common flowering plants, including trees

Working scientifically:

- observing closely, using simple equipment

Key vocabulary	
Tier 2 vocabulary:	**Tier 3 vocabulary:**
compare, describe, different, similar	group, identify, observe
adjectives to describe colour, shape, size, texture and smell	plant, roots

Health and safety Please refer to CLEAPSS for Health and Safety guidance and ensure that any identified hazards are managed appropriately.

Getting started

Remind children that they have been learning about the plant parts that grow above the ground and explain that today they are going to answer the question: **'What part of a plant grows under the ground?'**

Present Slideshow 1: Roots, slides 1–6. Ask children to point out the roots of these plants and to describe what they look like. Use this opportunity to remind children that the stems, roots and leaves grow above the ground and tell them that roots grow under the ground.

Now show slide 7. Ask children if they notice any similarities and differences between the roots. Ask them whether they can group them (place them into two groups).

Tell children that there are two types of roots: tap roots and branching roots.

(Note: a tap root is usually a single main root which grows deep into the ground. Sometimes there are smaller side roots which grow from it. Branching roots are networks of roots which are usually the same size and length. They grow more closely to the surface. Branching roots are often called fibrous roots, but there is no need to use this term in the lesson.)

Pupil workbook: Complete Activity 1: Drawing root vegetables on page 72.

The task

Tell children that they are going to observe one plant with a tap root and another with branching roots.

Give children some root vegetables such as carrots, radishes and beetroot (with tap roots). Ask them to make observational drawings of them as if they were in the ground. Ask children to add stems and leaves to their drawings.

Return to Slideshow 1: Roots. Show slides 8–10, which show the carrots, radishes and beetroot plants both on their own and growing in the ground. Ask children to compare their drawings with those from the slideshow.

Give children the pot plants. Model how to tease out the branching roots so that they are free and not covered in soil. Some roots will snap, especially if they are 'pot-bound' (have been in a small pot for too long) but this is not a problem. Ask children to loosen the soil from the roots so that they are visible. Ask children to describe to their partner what the branching roots look like. Ask children to observe how the roots are attached to the stem. Magnifiers could be used at this point.

When children have finished this activity, they could either re-pot the plant using the soil and larger pots or plant them somewhere in the school grounds.

Explain that plants are put in bigger pots or into the ground because this gives the roots more room to grow and that this allows the plant to grow larger.

If pot plants are unavailable, children could dig up 'weeds' from the school grounds that have been identified by the teacher.

These plants could be observed growing over the coming weeks.

Pupil workbook: Complete Activity 2: Tap roots and branching roots on page 73.

Adaptations and support

Some children may need support teasing out the branching roots from the pot plants. The teacher could complete this prior to the lesson and then place the plants back into the pot.

Take it further

Carrot tops could be placed on damp newspaper in a dish and left for a couple of weeks. Children can observe how stems and leaves grow from the tap root.

SNAP SCIENCE
GET YOUR TEETH INTO IT!
2nd EDITION

Reflect and review

Remind the children of the lesson question: **'What part of a plant grows under the ground?'** and that in this lesson they have been focusing on the roots of plants. They have learnt that all plants have roots which grow under the ground and that there are two types of roots: tap and branching.

Ask children what they did to help them answer the question. Confirm that they looked closely at the part of the plant that was under the ground. This is how scientists work, observing closely and systematically, and looking for similarities.

Ask children how they would explain to a gardener how they could find out whether their plants have tap roots or branching roots.

Answers

Plants with tap roots: dandelion, poppy and parsnip.

Plants with branching roots: pansy, petunia and geranium.

Homework suggestions

Children could look for root vegetables at home or in the supermarket. Which root vegetables do they like to eat? At this point accept any root vegetable which grows under the ground, including potatoes and yams which are actually swollen stems called tubers.

Assessment and evidence of learning

Children can:
- state that roots are the part of the plant which grow under the ground
- identify the differences and similarities between plants which have tap roots and those that have branching roots
- make accurate observational drawings of plants with tap and branching roots.

Lesson 4: Why are trees plants?

What children will learn and do

- Children learn that trees are plants.
- They observe evergreen and deciduous trees in their locality.
- They learn that trees have stems which are called trunks and that these are covered in bark.
- They notice that trees have leaves, roots and that most have flowers.
- They answer the lesson question: **'Why are trees plants?'**

You will need

- photographs of the trees studied in Module 1 Seasonal changes, Lesson 3
- paper and crayons for bark rubbings
- blindfolds (optional)

Ensure that the trees you will be visiting are in flower.

Snap Science Year 1 Pupil Workbook

- pages 74–75

Snap Science Year 1 Digital subscription

- Module 1, My Seasons Diary (children's copies already filled in)
- Slideshow 1: Trees
- Module 1, Lesson 1 Resource sheet 1: Leaf ID sheet

Make sure you have opened/printed any *Snap* resources you intend to use in this lesson.

National Curriculum

Conceptual knowledge:

- identify and name a variety of common wild and garden plants, including deciduous and evergreen trees
- identify and describe the basic structure of a variety of common flowering plants, including trees

Working scientifically:

- observing closely, using simple equipment
- identifying and classifying

Key vocabulary	
Tier 2 vocabulary:	**Tier 3 vocabulary:**
different adjectives to describe colour, shape, size, texture and smell	bark, deciduous, evergreen, flower, identify, leaf, plant, roots, stem, trunk

Health and safety Please refer to CLEAPSS for Health and Safety guidance and ensure that any identified hazards are managed appropriately.

Getting started

Some of this lesson will build upon the work covered in Module 1 Seasonal changes, and in particular, Lesson 3: Do all trees shed their leaves?

First, remind children of the trees they have already studied. Ask them whether they can name the two groups of trees (evergreen and deciduous). Ask them what these words mean.

Ask if children can name any of the trees that they looked at in the winter. Photographs of the trees that were taken in the winter could be used as a stimulus for this. Children can use their My Seasons Diary to remind themselves of the names of the trees and whether they are deciduous or evergreen. They could use their My Seasons Diaries to test each other or to help them identify the trees on slides 1–10 in Slideshow 1: Trees.

Then use slides 11–13 to show how evergreen and deciduous trees are different in the winter and the summer.

Ask children whether they think trees are plants. Ask them to explain why they think this. Tell them that today they are going to answer the lesson question: **'Why are trees plants?'**

Ask them to list the names of the parts of the plant that they have learnt about so far. They should be able to recall that plants have roots, stems, leaves, and most have flowers (and flower buds). Ask them whether they think trees have these plant parts.

Tell them that a tree has a stem and that it is called a trunk which is covered in bark. Tell them that many trees also have flowers which usually appear in the spring and summer.

Present slide 14 of Slideshow 1: Trees, and tell children that in some trees parts of the roots can be seen above the ground.

Then present slides 15–17 and ask children to identify where the flowers of each tree can be found.

Pupil workbook: Complete Activity 1: Deciduous or evergreen? on page 74.

The task

Take children out into the school grounds or the local park, and ask them to reuse Resource sheet 1: Leaf ID sheet from Module 1 Seasonal changes, Lesson 1, to identify and name the trees that have been selected for them. Children should choose one tree and describe to their partner whether they can see the roots of the tree and its flowers.

Model how to make a bark rubbing. When children have completed their own bark rubbings, they could swap rubbings with a partner and identify which tree the rubbing has been taken from. Children should use the tree's correct name to reinforce this learning.

Children could also 'meet a tree' blindfolded. They should work in pairs. Ask one child to take their blindfolded partner carefully to a tree and help them to feel the bark. The blindfolded child should then be led carefully away from the tree and spun around a couple of times. Ask the child to take their blindfold off and work out which tree they felt.

Pupil workbook: Complete Activity 2: Identifying trees on pages 74 and 75.

Adaptations and support

If children have difficulty holding the paper in place, masking tape can be used while children make their rubbings.

Take it further

A range of flowers from trees could be provided for close observation. These could be compared with some of the flowers studied in Lessons 1 and 2. Some tree flowers have fairly insignificant flowers which are small and pale, such as oak and beech tree catkins. Ask children if they can spot any of these.

Reflect and review

Remind the children of the lesson question: **'Why are trees plants?'** and that in this lesson they have been focusing on the features that trees have which make them plants: trunk/stem, leaves, roots and flowers.

Explain that children have worked like scientists, by recording their observations.

Ask children to draw a tree and label it with 'roots', 'trunk (stem)', 'leaves' and 'flowers'.

Pupil workbook: Complete Activity 3: Parts of a tree on page 75.

Answers

Evergreen trees are trees that keep their leaves through the winter. These trees continually shed and replace their leaves throughout the year.

Deciduous trees are trees whose leaves change colour in the autumn and fall off and by the winter the tree has no leaves on its branches.

Trees are plants. They have roots, stems and leaves. Most have flowers. Some trees such as fir trees are non-flowering plants and do not produce flowers, but cones instead.

Homework suggestions

On their walk home from school, children could find trees which have flowers so that they can describe to the rest of the class where they found the trees and what the flowers looked like.

Assessment and evidence of learning

Children can:
- use the senses of touch and sight
- state that trees are also plants because they have stems, roots, leaves and flowers
- state that the stem of a tree is called a trunk, and that trunks are covered in bark
- label different tree parts as 'roots', 'stem/trunk', 'leaves' and 'flowers'
- identify trees using pictures of leaves.

Lesson 5: What are the similarities and differences between plants that have flowers?

What children will learn and do

- Children name and compare the parts of different plants.
- They design their own plant including the correct parts.
- They answer the lesson question: **'What are the similarities and differences between plants that have flowers?'**

You will need

- paper, glue and scissors (optional)

If using the Snap Science Year 1 Pupil Workbook you may not require the resource sheet below.

Snap Science Year 1 Pupil Workbook

- pages 76–77

Snap Science Year 1 Digital subscription

- Slideshow 1: Comparing plant parts
- Resource sheet 1: Plant parts
- Snapshot 1: Name that plant!
- Snapshot 2: Name that part!

Make sure you have opened/printed any *Snap* resources you intend to use in this lesson.

National Curriculum

Conceptual knowledge:

- identify and describe the basic structure of a variety of common flowering plants, including trees

Working scientifically:

- identifying and classifying

Key vocabulary	
Tier 2 vocabulary:	**Tier 3 vocabulary:**
compare, describe, different, similar	group, identify
adjectives to describe colour, shape, size, texture and smell	bark, flower, leaf, plant, roots, stem, trunk

Health and safety Please refer to CLEAPSS for Health and Safety guidance and ensure that any identified hazards are managed appropriately.

Getting started

Tell children that they are going to think about what they have learnt about plants during this block of learning, and answer the question: **'What are the similarities and differences between plants that have flowers?'**

Ask: What parts do all plants have? Which parts of the plant grow above or under the ground?

Present Slideshow 1: Comparing plant parts. Tell children that they are going to compare leaves, stems, roots and flowers from different plants. Ask them to describe what is similar and different about the parts of the plants that are shown. Remind them: that the stem of a tree is called a trunk and it is covered in bark; that plants can be grouped into those that have a tap root and those that have branching roots; that not all flowers are large and brightly coloured and that some plants, like nettles, have flowers which are small and pale.

During this process you should create a word bank from the children's responses. These words can be used by the children when describing the plant that they will design in the following activity.

The task

Ask children to design their own plant, based on the plant parts that they like the best from Resource sheet 1: Plant parts. They should choose roots, stems, leaves and flowers from the options on each page. They could either draw or cut out these plant parts to design their plant. Ask them to label their drawings with the following key vocabulary: stem/trunk, leaf, branching roots/tap root, flower, above the ground, under the ground. In addition to this they should label which plant each part has come from.

Then ask children to describe their designed plant to their partner. Their partner should identify the name of the plant that each part has come from. Using the word bank, children should then compare their plants, describing how they are similar and different.

Pupil workbook: Complete Activity 1: Designing a plant on page 76.

Adaptations and support

Plant parts could already be cut out for children. Rather than a written label, children could point to and state the plant part.

Take it further

Children could find out about carnivorous plants such as the Venus fly trap and pitcher plants.

Reflect and review

Remind the children of the lesson question: **'What are the similarities and differences between plants that have flowers?'** and that in this lesson they have remembered all the things they have learnt about plants.

The teacher could design their own plant and describe it to the class so that children can identify the plants it has been made from. Alternatively, Resource sheet 1: Plant parts could be presented to the class and specific plant parts selected by the teacher. Children should then describe the allocated plant part.

Pupil workbook: Complete Activity 2: Describing plant parts on page 77.

Answers

Different types of plant are similar because they have roots, stems, leaves, and most have flowers, but these look different on different plants.

Homework suggestions

Children could take their designed plant home and describe it to a friend or family member who has to identify the plants that it is made up of.

Assessment and evidence of learning

Children can:
- state that plants are made up of roots, stems and leaves, and that most have flowers
- state that stems, leaves and flowers can be found above the ground and roots below the ground
- state that trees are plants because they also have these plant parts
- state that the stem of a tree is called a trunk
- include the correct parts and label their own plants correctly
- use descriptive language (colour, shape, size, texture and smell) to compare the roots, stems, leaves and flowers of different plants
- identify the different plants parts of a made up plant has come from.

SNAP
SCIENCE
GET YOUR TEETH INTO IT!
2nd EDITION

If you are unsure if a child can identify and name a variety of common wild and garden plants, including deciduous and evergreen trees, you can use the Snapshot activity: Name that plant!

If you are unsure if a child can identify and describe the basic structure of a variety of common flowering plants, including trees, you can use the Snapshot activity: Name that part!